Praise for

New Life After Divorce

"When divorce drains you of hope, this book can refill you with encouragement, optimism, and plans for a brighter future. My friend Bill Butterworth isn't an armchair pontificator; his wise and biblical advice flows out of his own heartbreak and new life. Let your journey toward recovery begin now!"

—LEE STROBEL, author of *The Case for Christ* and *The Case for a Creator*

"If you're divorced, then you're in the club—The Walking Wounded Club—where a lifetime membership came wrapped in a broken heart. Come to these words and hear about the only One who is able to carry the wounded—our merciful God, who heals and restores and redeems. He is the God of Glory, and He promises to make your broken life new."

—ANGELA THOMAS, speaker and author of *Do You Think I'm Beautiful?*

"Bill Butterworth's *New Life After Divorce* is a channel of God's love to people in pain. Divorce breaks God's heart and the hearts of its victims, but Bill reminds us through his own vulnerability that it happens—even in the church. By reading *New Life After Divorce,* you'll be assured that hope can live again, even when you think it can't."

—THOM LEMMONS, author of *Jabez*

"Bill takes you through an honest journey of life after divorce, providing you with encouragement, hope, and practical suggestions for personal growth and healing."

—Dr. Roger Tirabassi, pastoral counselor

"*New Life After Divorce* is a light for an often dark path. Bill Butterworth's honesty, humor, and vision for the future provide practical direction as well as graceful encouragement for those going through the difficulties of divorce. Thank you, Bill, for this much-needed handbook of hope!"

—Sharon Hersh, author of *"Mom, Everyone Else Does!"* and *"Mom, I Hate My Life!"*

"Many know Bill Butterworth as a master communicator and humorist. In *New Life After Divorce* you will come to know him as a friend who walks humbly, authentically, and candidly with those who know firsthand the ugly reality of marriage breakdown and who wonder if there is any hope for their future. Bill has lived each word of this book. You will find life in every page."

—Gene Appel, associate pastor, Willow Creek Community Church

New Life
after divorce

New Life

after divorce

the promise of hope beyond the pain

Bill Butterworth

WATERBROOK
PRESS

NEW LIFE AFTER DIVORCE
PUBLISHED BY WATERBROOK PRESS
2375 Telstar Drive, Suite 160
Colorado Springs, Colorado 80920
A division of Random House, Inc.

Details in some anecdotes and stories have been changed to protect the identities of the persons involved.

ISBN 1-4000-7095-3

Published in association with the literary agency of Alive Communications, Inc., 7680 Goddard Street, Suite 200, Colorado Springs, CO 80920.

Library of Congress Cataloging-in-Publication Data
Butterworth, Bill.
  New life after divorce : the promise of hope beyond the pain / Bill Butterworth.— 1st ed.
    p. cm.
  ISBN 1-4000-7095-3
  1. Divorced people—Religious life. 2. Divorce—Religious aspects—Christianity. I. Title.
  BV4596.D58B88 2005
  248.8'46—dc22

                                        2004028941

Printed in the United States of America
2005—First Edition

10 9 8 7 6 5 4 3 2 1

This book is dedicated to
Ken and Mari Harrower
and
Bill Flanagan,
three professionals and three good friends
who helped Kathi and me process the pain
and taught us that there is
new life after divorce.
We can never thank you enough.

Contents

Part Four: The Ultimate Issues

Foreword

Somebody said a long time ago that God never wastes a hurt. A theological term for this is redemption. A practical expression of this is the work you hold in your hand.

Some books are written to entertain, others to intrigue. Some are abstract discussions of theoretical issues. Writers are never sure what kind of readers will pick up these books. But this book is different. If you are reading these words, this topic is probably not some distant and vague subject for you. Maybe you have been through divorce yourself. Maybe it has touched someone you love. Maybe you're standing on shaky ground and wondering what the future holds. But most likely you are not picking up this book out of idle curiosity.

In the mysterious alchemy that divine redemption brings about, Bill has been given both the gifts and the scars needed to write this book. He is one of the most gifted communicators around. Lots of people can inform; Bill can touch the heart. His ability to move people to laughter and tears means he can get the scalpel of healing deeply into the soul before you even realize what he's up to.

In addition to that, he has a searching love for God's Word. He has the theological training and education to be able to address a difficult and complex subject with clear, biblical thinking.

He also has the experience that comes from conversations around a thousand cups of coffee with people at camps or conferences or retreats, when they are most ready to open up. He has heard the cries and the evasions and the hopes of the human heart.

And—he has walked through the valley himself. He knows from the inside the devastation, the guilt, the regret, the self-consciousness, the longings, the memories, the dryness, the fragile hopes, the persistence required, and the power of grace received on the long road to healing.

From the outside, divorce can sound like a single event. But anyone who has ever experienced it knows that it is an earthquake that rearranges every part of the landscape—emotions, identity, finances, spirituality, parenthood, vocation, recreation, and friendships. If it is true that every divorce is the death of a small civilization, then its aftermath requires the construction of a new one. All of this, Bill knows. All of this, Bill feels.

And so this is not as much a book as it is a lifeline. One of the difficulties of divorce is that it demands so much *thinking,* so many choices to be made, at a time when a person's capacity for such things is being drained like never before. Bill speaks of how to navigate these demands with a graceful and gritty reality that will be enormously helpful.

It would be hard to name a time when people need sane, biblical guidance more than when they have been through the pain of a divorce. It would be hard to name a better, wiser, gentler, truer guide than Bill Butterworth. God will use him and this book to bring hope and healing to many.

—John Ortberg
teaching pastor, Menlo Park
Presbyterian Church

Acknowledgments

The men and women at WaterBrook Press are fantastic. When I first shared the idea for this book with *Don Pape*, his enthusiasm was contagious. *Bruce Nygren* helped with important editing insights, and many of the staff read the entire manuscript and offered wise improvements.

Lee Hough, my literary agent, not only provided agency representation for me but also contributed additional keen observations regarding this project.

One of the biggest blessings I have been currently experiencing is the friendship that has developed with *Lee Strobel*. Our weekly lunches have become a high point and are always filled with genuine encouragement.

Steve Arterburn and the whole gang at New Life Ministry have also provided great encouragement regarding this project, and for that I am truly appreciative.

My pastor and friend, *Kenton Beshore*, is a constant source of energy and hope. All the folks at Mariners Church deserve hearty thanks for their uplifting contribution to my life.

And, of course, I get to meet dozens of ministers by being invited to speak at their churches, and I have met the cream of the crop. I offer deep appreciation to men who believe in me—men like *Bill Hybels, Rick Warren, John Ortberg, Ray Johnston, Stu Boehmig, Jud Wilhite, Mark Bankord,* and *Rene Schlaepfer,* just to name a few.

There are some I must acknowledge as long-term friends. These are the folks who helped me through the dark days of my divorce. Thanks to *Joe Davis, Mike Scott, Ron Nelson, Gary Bender, Bob Ludwig, Ken Gire,* and *Ed*

Neuenschwander. I wouldn't be here today if it weren't for your love and support.

My five children are off-the-chart amazing. They have been as supportive of my journey as any five people could be. I thank God every day for my daughter, *Joy,* her husband, *Justin,* my little granddaughter, *Jill,* my son *Jesse,* his wife, *Marisa,* my little grandson, *Liam,* and my sons *Jeffrey, John,* and *Joseph.* I love you with all of my heart.

The story of my divorce is a painful one, but another chapter was to be written. I met my wife *Kathi,* who has become the dearest, sweetest, love-of-my-life best friend a guy could ask for. Thank You, God, for this gracious gift.

And thank You, *Heavenly Father,* for all the relationships You have blessed me with in my life. May this book bring glory to You.

New Life
after divorce

Part One

The Basics

I Need Acceptance
from Myself

I WAS A MAN who thought he had it all.

I had a wife of seventeen years, five beautiful kids, a rising career, and ever-increasing financial security. For the first six years of our marriage, I taught on the faculty of a private college. Then I became a counselor on the staff of a well-respected radio program and eventually developed into a full-time speaker and writer on issues of marriage and family. Life made sense, and I had it all figured out in the grand scheme of things.

But it all changed in 1993.

My marriage ended in divorce.

Let's get it straight from the start: I'm not condoning what happened in my life. I'm not trying to place myself on a pedestal as a guy who once struggled and is now "all better." Just when I think I've worked it all through, the struggles can revisit on a moment's notice. This is not an essay written to mar the character or integrity of my former wife. No, this isn't about her. It's about ME.

When the divorce happened, my world came crashing down. Some of my friends compared their divorces to being shot in the gut with a pistol. Mine felt like a one-two blast from a double-barreled shotgun. Not only was I blown away by the loss of the most treasured human relationship I had experienced, but the second shot blew me apart vocationally. Few groups wanted someone who was divorced to speak on marriages.

I felt like a Lexus dealer driving a Dodge Dart.

I did not work for six months. My debt grew every day. I felt I was no good to anybody, and I struggled to get out of bed in the morning. I was a divorced, unemployed, sorry excuse for a man. So I did what any male would do in a similar situation.

I hid.

"No one is going to know my pain or embarrassment," I concluded. "I will go under cover." I became adept at dodging questions, avoiding eye contact, and changing the subject. People knew something was wrong, but I kept convincing myself they didn't. I was desperately lonely, deeply depressed, and committed to a classic case of denial. I lived each day waiting for the phone to ring, hoping my wife would say she wanted to get back together.

That phone call never came…

Does any of this travail sound familiar? My sense is that you wouldn't be perusing the pages of this book if it didn't. But maybe you are a professional who is looking to be of further help to divorced people in your group. Or perhaps you've been divorced for quite a while, and many of the wounds have healed or at least scabbed over. But I am imagining that the vast majority of readers eying these words are right in the thick of it. You've never hurt more than you hurt right now. Things that once made sense are spinning around in circles seemingly out of control.

This book is for you. I want this to be a realistic look at what's going on so that you understand *you are not alone* in your feelings. All of us who have endured the end of our marriages know the pain you are experiencing.

In the midst of the stress you feel, I want these pages to bring *encouragement and hope.* You will get through it. I know you don't feel that way right now, but trust me, you'll make it.

Self-Acceptance

So let's begin at the most basic level. If you're like most single-agains, you may be less than happy about your place in life. Being lumped into the category of the "divorced" leaves you uneasy, unsettled, and embarrassed. This book is not written to address the gory details that led up to your divorce. It's not about who is at fault and why. It's about where you are *now.* What happened in the past is helpful only as we can learn lessons from it. We're not going to dwell on the past in this book but rather look to the future.

The most important step you can take to begin adjusting to your new life is to *accept it.* Trust me, it is a lot easier to write about than to actually accomplish, but it can happen.

Centuries ago King Solomon wrapped self-acceptance into one concise statement: "As he thinks within himself, so he is" (Proverbs 23:7).

You are what you think you are! If you think you're a no-good, dirty, rotten bum, that's the way you will live your life. Others will begin treating you that same way, because every signal you send them asks for that kind of treatment. Likewise, if I have a positive self-image, if I feel good about myself, this message will also translate to others, and they will respond appropriately.

Many of us struggled with low self-esteem *before* divorce entered our lives. The end of our marriages just feels like piling on. All of us deal with a level of insecurity, but some of us struggle more than others. As a child I viewed myself as the little fat kid that everyone else picked on. To my disservice, when I grew to be a man, I still tended to see myself the same way. Add a divorce to the equation, and I was convinced it all added up to a LOSER. Consider this embarrassing slice from my life's pity pie.

THE VALENTINE'S DAY MASSACRE

As a married man I always looked forward to February 14. I enjoyed the challenge of making each Valentine's Day a little different and better than the one before. It was a tailor-made occasion for lovers that created fond memories.

But when I became single again, February 14 took on a whole different feeling. The best spin I could put on it was that it was different than past celebrations. Because there was no celebration.

My first year as a single-again man, I agreed to do consulting work for a friend. Several of us made arrangements to meet in the mountains for a planning session. Because February 14 would fall in the middle of the three-day meeting, I hoped I would be too preoccupied to give it much thought, although I knew several of the men would bring their wives.

I arrived the night of the thirteenth at a beautiful mountain resort in Colorado. The next morning, as the sun came up, I walked out of my room onto the balcony. A brilliant blue sky framed the snowcapped mountains and stately evergreens. I drew in a breath of cool, crisp air and longed to have someone with whom to share this awesome moment. But I put the thought quickly from my mind and turned to begin the day.

Our think tank proved productive. By seven o'clock that evening we had accomplished more than we expected. My friend glanced at his watch and announced, "Oh no. I told my wife I would take her out for Valentine's Day dinner. I gotta run, or I'll be in big trouble."

Several other guys joined him going out the door. Within three minutes the entire circle of men cleared out, leaving me and one other guy named Randy sitting by ourselves.

We looked at each other in silence for a few moments. Then Randy's face lit up as he said, "I hear they have a great restaurant here. Let me take a minute to call my wife back home, then what do you say we go downstairs and throw ourselves a little party?"

Sounded good to me. Randy was sad because he had to be away from his wife, and I was sad because I didn't have a wife to be away from. We were an exciting duo.

After he made his phone call, we threw on our suit coats and walked downstairs to the restaurant. Randy walked up to the maître d' and asked for a table for two. "Well of course, sir. Tonight we have nothing *but* tables for two."

He led us toward the most coveted table in the room, right next to a majestic old fireplace complete with a crackling fire. As we followed the maître d', I couldn't help but notice the turned heads and whispers. I checked to see if my shirttail was hanging out or my zipper was down.

After I sat down, I realized we had the only table in the entire restaurant that wasn't occupied by a male-and-female Valentine's Day couple! A hostess made the rounds, presenting each lovely lady with a red rose. When she arrived at our table, she cleared her throat and asked, "Which one of you would like the rose?"

"Not me," an embarrassed Randy instantaneously replied. "We're here from out of town. I'm from Texas. *He's* from California."

He pointed to me as he said the word *California.* The room grew silent, and I felt as if that one word provided the necessary explanation for the entire situation.

By now Randy and I were sweating like pigs. "Gee, it's kinda warm here by the fire," I said lamely, attempting casual conversation. It wasn't working. We wiped perspiration from our foreheads with pink linen napkins.

The waiter approached us. "Tell us about your specials this evening, my good man!" I said, trying to remove the awkwardness of the moment and focus on the main reason we were there—food. It was the wrong question to ask.

"Tonight all our specials are dinners for *two.* We will start you off with champagne and then toss an elegant Caesar salad for two right at your table. The entrée of your choice comes next in a double portion. We follow it with one of our famous flaming desserts."

"I'll take the biggest steak you have!" Randy interrupted loud enough for all the diners to hear. He had heard enough about dinners for two. Apparently, he felt it was an appropriate strategy to reestablish himself as a Texan who lived off meat and potatoes.

"I'll take the same thing," I said when it was my turn. Randy shot me a glance of disappointment, so I hastily changed my order. "No, make mine a prime rib."

"King's cut or queen's, sir?" our waiter asked.

"King's cut. Definitely. King's cut."

When the waiter left our table, we both laughed nervously at our situation. "My wife's never gonna believe this!" Randy confessed, twisting his napkin into a tight knot.

We continued our vain attempts at conversation. Although Randy grew more comfortable as the dinner progressed, I sat ramrod straight the whole evening. We asked our waiter to bring the check as soon as the entrées arrived.

Two men have never put away food more quickly than the two of us. We scarfed down our meal, replaced our pink napkins on the table, and stood to leave. As we walked out, Randy said loudly, "I'm going back to my hotel room. See you tomorrow for the *business* meeting."

I went back to my room, threw off my coat, and nearly choked myself taking off my tie. Throwing myself across the bed, I buried my head in the pillow and cried like a baby. The silent room intensified the sounds of my weeping. But inside my heart I was screaming at the top of my lungs: *Why did I have to be the one person in the whole stinking restaurant without a valentine? Why did it have to be my marriage that failed?*

I've had lots of time to reflect since that Valentine's Day evening many years ago. I have come to realize how easy it is to use disappointments as an opportunity for self-pity. On one hand, we need freedom to work through the grieving process (which we will look at more extensively in chapter 4). But if we are not careful, our grief can sidetrack us into a full-blown pity party, complete with all the sadness and depression that accompany it.

It was also during this time that I came face to face with a biblical principle I'd never needed to wrestle with before. It centers around Paul's words in Philippians: "Not that I speak from want, for I have learned to be content in whatever circumstances I am" (Philippians 4:11).

Contentment is a difficult concept to grasp in our hard-driving culture.

We say we are content, but our lifestyles speak differently. If we were truly content, we wouldn't worry as we do. We wouldn't be as driven. We wouldn't keep struggling with the same feelings of inadequacy and dissatisfaction.

I *talked* contentment on previous Valentine's Days, but on this one I was experiencing what it was like to live in want. I wanted the old days back: fun and freedom and love and companionship and unity and affection and sunshine.

But life took a different turn.

So, like many others I know, I have learned what it means to be content. It is about acceptance; the more I accept what is happening in my life and seek to learn from it, the more progress I make.

I still had many days of yearning for the past and the life I had planned for my family and me. That's not an evil thing. It's not falling off the wagon or regressing. It's real life.

But part of achieving contentment comes from making progress. I make a little more every day. I now am grateful to God for bringing situations into my life that teach me truths I need to learn. I am developing a better understanding of acceptance, contentment, and peace.

So how do I work on self-esteem? I stop beating myself up! But won't that lead to an unhealthy view of myself from the other extreme? What can I do to distinguish between behaviors I don't like in my life and the whole issue of unconditional acceptance? These are valid questions. I believe the answer is found in the bear hug.

THE BEAR HUG

We are a family of huggers. Whether it's the two-year-old toddler of yesterday or the twenty-seven-year-old who can pick me up today, hugging has a special place for the Butterworths. So allow a little family anecdote to illustrate a personal point of application.

We call our most intimate hugs bear hugs. (We also refer to them by the more crass title "squeezing your guts out.") They are special hugs we share when we've returned from a long trip, landed straight A's, or learned to do something new. The bear hug has become more than a physical act of kindness in our home. It has evolved into a symbol of the sort of love we want to characterize our family life.

One of the arms I place around my children is the arm of *acceptance*. It is known by its unconditional nature. It's another way of saying to the kids, "I love you. Nothing can take that love away. Nothing."

A parent might desire for his child to be first chair with his clarinet, but his child doesn't have the musical goods. Barely making the fourth-grade band by the skin of his clarinet reed, this child is musically challenged. The band is playing "The Star-Spangled Banner," and this kid is playing "Lightly Row." I like to call a little guy like this "outstandingly average." So what does a parent do?

Give him a big ol' bear hug while whispering, "I love you with all my heart. It doesn't matter if you earn all A's, score the winning goal, or trill right off the staff. I will love you forever!"

But a one-armed hug is incomplete. Unlike the unconditional nature of the arm of acceptance, the arm of *approval* is built on conditions.

It says, "I will always love you, but we have certain guidelines in our home to keep it running smoothly. When you violate those rules, there will be a price to pay. Reaping the consequences of your actions is another way our relationship is defined."

The two-armed bear hug eliminates the heart-wrenching scenario of a child's having to earn a parent's love. The beauty of it is that the person hugged sees there are standards that must be upheld. At the same time, the individual never mistakes those accomplishments as a way of earning love.

Both the arm of acceptance and the arm of approval are invigorated by another person's energy as it transfers through the correct squeeze. A hug so hard that it takes the breath away has to originate from strength.

This strength does not come from pumping iron. It comes only from God. It comes from being grounded in a relationship with Him. It's the outgrowth of being rooted in His Scriptures. It's the fruit of those times we spend in prayer, asking Him for help in accepting ourselves, getting on with our lives, and raising our children so they will grow up to look like Him. Those sorts of activities produce strong bear hugs.

Look at what God says about *you*, His unique and gifted child:

> Therefore I urge you, brethren, by the mercies of God, to present your bodies a living and holy sacrifice, acceptable to God, which is your spiritual service of worship. And do not be conformed to this world, but be transformed by the renewing of your mind, so that you may prove what the will of God is, that which is good and acceptable and perfect.
>
> For through the grace given to me I say to everyone among you not to think more highly of himself than he ought to think; but to think so as to have sound judgment, as God has allotted to each a measure of faith. For just as we have many members in one body and all the members do not have the same function, so we, who are many, are one body in Christ, and individually members one of another. Since we have gifts that differ according to the grace given to us, each of us is to exercise them accordingly. (Romans 12:1–6)

This passage is loaded with gems. Each of us is given gifts by God's grace. You may not be feeling real gifted at this juncture in life, but your feelings notwithstanding, you have talents and abilities given you by the Lord. Just as Paul told us not to think more highly of ourselves than we ought to think, a case can be made for avoiding the other extreme as well. Don't think less of yourself than you ought to think. God has gifted you, and you are one of His unique creations.

The verses tell us we are unique. Just as a human body has many parts, each with a different function, the body of Christ is the same. You have something to contribute in life, something positive, something necessary. I remember being in a room full of friends telling me this very message and realizing I was the only guy in the room who didn't get what they were saying—and they were talking about me!

The bottom line on all this hugging stuff is that the bear hug has to be experienced in its entirety. Receiving the arm of acceptance alone leads to an undisciplined, unstructured relationship reminiscent of a bowl of Jell-O. The arm of approval on its own gives a kid the impression that he or she is being raised by a military dictator. But the arms of acceptance and approval, given together, can accomplish great things.

Okay, so much for my advice on a good way to raise kids. Here's my point for you: *have you balanced the issues of acceptance and approval in your own life?* You know what I mean. Are you confusing acceptance and approval as you deal with your life as a single-again adult? Are you still beating yourself up for the shortcomings that surfaced as a result of your divorce? Granted, seasons of life like the one you're in now provide an excellent opportunity for self-reflection and self-improvement, but some of us have to give ourselves a break! We've slapped ourselves silly, and it's no wonder we can't function—we've made ourselves punch-drunk.

So you don't like where you are right now? That's understandable. It's time for a dose of self-acceptance, however. Let your eyes run over the following statement several times:

I accept who I am, including being a divorced person, for I know God loves me, accepts me, and will continue to use me for good things in life.

In other words, go ahead, give yourself a big bear hug. Squeeze your guts out.

I Need Healing from God

Okay, so I am working on accepting myself, even though I have the nagging thought that I am considered a second-class citizen because of this divorce. Nonetheless, I am attempting to apply the truth of chapter 1. I need to accept myself.

But there's still a void in my life. A hole deep inside yearns to be healed and made whole. My divorce was the most intense pain I had ever felt. It was so hurtful that I was unable to bounce back as I had done in other situations. I needed healing, and as we shall discover in this chapter, ultimate healing comes from God.

It's More Than I Can Handle

To know my friend Sammy was to know a man who had it all together. Blessed with extraordinary good looks, Sammy was as bright as he was handsome, and his intelligence played itself out in the world of business.

Sammy led a charmed life. After graduating at the top of his class at a major university, he parlayed that accomplishment into getting accepted into an MBA program at one of the most prestigious business schools in the country. Upon graduating from it, he was heavily recruited by Fortune 100 business firms nationwide. He made his choice, went to work, and along the way met a beautiful young woman. Stephanie was every bit as much a catch as Sammy was. They married after dating about two years.

They had a storybook life. Sammy made good money and rose quickly in the company. He rose so fast that he soon took his knowledge and experience and started his own company. It was as close to an instant success as one could imagine.

On the home front, Stephanie was pregnant with twins. It wasn't a particularly difficult pregnancy, but she was experiencing a greater need for Sammy's help around the house at a time when his new business was pulling him even harder in the other direction. Steph or the business? Sammy chose the new company. Consequently, bitterness and resentment built up inside of Stephanie.

Brittany and Brooke were born a few months later, and for a while the joy of the new little ones hid the anger and frustration that Stephanie held deep below the surface. Sammy tried to be home more, but it turned out to be too little too late. The more Sammy hung out at the house, the more Stephanie used it as an excuse to get out. "Why are you always leaving when I arrive?" he would ask her.

"You have no idea what it's like to be cooped up here all day with two infants. Just cover for me while I unwind with my girlfriends."

Sammy suspected that these trips out were more than visits with girlfriends. Ultimately he confronted her, and she admitted the whole painful soap opera.

"You're right, Sammy. I've met someone else. He is the most attentive man I have ever known. You had your chance, and you blew it. I could never forgive you for how you abandoned me when I needed you. So now I am getting on with my life. I've hired a lawyer, who is drawing up divorce papers even as we speak. I was going to tell you tomorrow, but you beat me to it, just as you always do. It's your way or the highway—and you probably don't even realize that's what you're communicating. I'm sick of it, and I'm leaving. We'll make sure you have lots of time with the twins, but you and I are history."

"When Stephanie left, my world came crashing down," Sammy now recalls. "The guy who had been known as the one who could always hold it together came apart at the seams. I didn't have a clue about how to save this broken marriage. I couldn't even figure out a logical way to do damage control. It was more than I could handle."

And with those words, Sammy, the original self-dependent man, found the need for the Lord in his life. "My mother made me go to church when I was a kid," he remembers. "But I hated it. It was a mixture of the most boring sermons I had ever heard and the biggest bunch of hypocrites ever assembled. As soon as I was old enough to make up my own mind, church was erased as an option, even for Sunday mornings. There were more important things to do.

"But about forty-eight hours after Steph packed up and left with the babies, I got a call from a buddy of mine. We had worked together at the big firm before I left and started my own company. Brad said he was just checking in, but the phone call showed the miraculous timing of God."

"So what's new, Sammy?" Brad had asked innocently enough.

"Well, business has never been better, but my personal life is in the tank," Sammy replied honestly. With that intro, Sammy told Brad all the gory details of the impending divorce. "I'm usually not that transparent," Sammy reflects, "but when you've come to the end of your rope, you tend to open up to other options."

Brad responded to Sammy in a way that initially jolted him. "He invited me to attend church with him," Sammy remembers. "He offered to swing by and pick me up on Saturday night if I was free (which I was), and after church we'd go to a great Mexican restaurant in town. I couldn't refuse, which still amazes me. Normally, I could shut down an invitation like that in a heartbeat. But I had run out of options, and somehow church sounded like the right thing to do."

Brad took Sammy to his church the following Saturday night, and Sammy was in for a big surprise. He had never experienced a church with a band instead of a choir and organ. They even had a drama team, which acted out a tale of a life falling apart. But at the end of the drama, the young actress recalled her spiritual roots and called on God to help her find her way through all this tragedy.

"The drama hit me hard," Sammy recalls. "First of all, I could totally identify with the girl whose life was falling apart. But I had no spiritual heritage to fall back on. I was just about weeping when the pastor stood up to begin his message.

"He spoke about a man who had been sick for thirty-eight years yet somehow believed a pool outside the city would heal him. Jesus showed up and healed the guy right on the spot. God did what no human or circumstance could do. It was all about trusting Him to heal us.

Brad and Sammy left the church and headed for the Mexican cantina. "Naturally the conversation was all about the pastor's message and my current situation," Sammy recounts. "Brad helped me understand that

God loves *me*—something I had never imagined. When Jesus died on the cross, He did it for me—to pay for all my mess and hurt and pain. I wanted to know that kind of forgiveness and power and, most of all, healing in my life. I know it doesn't sound very spiritual, but I silently prayed and asked Jesus to be my personal Savior that night right there at the Mexican cantina over chips and salsa. Actually Brad helped lead me in the prayer, and we got interrupted halfway through by the waitress with our burritos!"

Sammy needed more than acceptance from himself and help from others. He needed healing, and that can come only from God. "It wasn't something magical that changed everything overnight," Sammy explains honestly. "There were still mountains of problems to overcome. But the beautiful thing is that God helped heal the gut-wrenching pain deep inside of me. I felt like I mattered to Him, even if I didn't matter to my wife. Humanly speaking, I owe a great deal to Brad, who helped me through this entire ordeal. He got me plugged into a men's group. [We'll talk about how important that is in a subsequent chapter.] He even saw to it that I enrolled in a divorce recovery program at a big church down the road. It was so beneficial to me that I volunteered to be a helper in their future sessions, and now it's a regular part of my life. To help people find the healing that God brings to life is one of the greatest joys I have ever experienced. It's a greater rush than signing the big deal or reeling in the new client."

Adjusting the Focus

Sammy's story may sound like your story or may be quite different. Unlike Sammy, some folks drift from their spiritual roots during times of crisis.

But in his case, as in my own journey, I drew closer to the Lord. Sammy and I have different points of connection, however, since I had known the Lord personally from the time I was a teenager. But I was equally devastated when my marriage ended. I knew from long ago that God doesn't promise a life free of pain, but He does promise us a way to deal with the pain and His healing power to ultimately rise above it.

Concerned friends could see my pain, and they shared with me the comforting words of Jeremiah: " 'For I know the plans that I have for you,' declares the LORD, 'plans to prosper you and not to harm you, plans to give you hope and a future. Then you will call upon me and come and pray to me, and I will listen to you. You will seek me and find me when you seek me with all your heart' " (Jeremiah 29:11–13, NIV).

Thanks to God, healing did come into my life as time passed. And I learned quite a few spiritual lessons in the process. I learned to seek God in a renewed way, and He brought His plan, His future, and His hope. As I watched this progress, my pattern of worship changed. I had always participated actively in the Sunday morning service but usually as a quiet observer. I would sing softly at my place in the pew, close my eyes during prayers, and listen attentively to the sermon.

But during my darkest days I discovered the wonder and healing of worship. I slipped into the back row of our church and sang louder than I had ever sung, until my voice cracked with emotion. I listened to the pastor's sermon, and through it I realized God still rules and is at work healing His wounded warriors.

I also became aware of His attention to my pride. He saw my self-sufficient mind-set, created during the comfortable years, and He changed the game plan. I saw how easy it was to neglect God when things were going well. The withdrawal of some of those gifts forced me to refocus on the Giver rather than the gifts.

Proverbs 18:12 states it this way: "Before his downfall a man's heart is proud, but humility comes before honor" (NIV).

God loved me enough to humble me, though I can still revert to proud thoughts when things are going well, and I am convinced it is a lesson I will always be learning. But God helped me realize anew that *everything* I have in this life comes from His hands.

INSTRUCTION VERSUS ENCOUNTER

Becoming a divorced person was the furthest thing from my mind when I began working in ministry almost twenty years earlier. I knew people who were in this situation, but I could only give them counsel learned from textbooks. When I think back to those days, I know I shared some things that were helpful, but I also said a lot that showed I had no clue what it was really like.

Why would I have any insight into loneliness? I was a happily married man. Financial stress? I was my making my way up the money ladder. Rejection? I remembered being rejected by a girl who didn't like me in the ninth grade; that's like comparing a scab to a tumor.

Then I read a verse in the book of Job that I had read before, but this time it took on a whole new meaning. "My ears had heard of you but now my eyes have seen you" (Job 42:5, NIV).

What was the difference between Job's hearing and seeing? *The experiencing of his pain.* Notice the reference of the verse? It's at the end of the book of Job, after he has personally endured pain and suffering. Just as Job more deeply understood life as a result of suffering, so it is with folks like you and me who go through tragic situations.

THE CHRISTMAS GIFT

Christmas had always been my favorite time of year—a blending of my most significant treasures: God and my family. We worked hard at pioneering Christmas traditions, from birthday cakes for baby Jesus to organizing the neighborhood Christmas caroling.

But my first Christmas as a newly divorced guy was brutal. What had always been the highlight of the year was now an awkward occasion of negotiating—who had whom for when until when and how to keep Christmas special for the kids.

I became a brokenhearted wreck. I resented the holiday's commercialism, and I longed to use that as an excuse for not celebrating at all. I remember telling my kids a comment I had heard years before from a seminary professor: "Baby Jesus was most likely born in a cave, since that is where farm animals were kept at that time in history." I could just imagine their horrified stares at my announcement: "Therefore we will have a very Spartan Christmas this year. No gifts, no trees, no tinsel or wrapping. Remember, kids, Jesus was born in a cave."

But I just couldn't do it.

I wanted my children to have as normal a Christmas as possible, so I decided to drag myself through the motions.

On the Sunday before Christmas, I walked into the sanctuary of our church having no idea what was about to take place. The room was warmly decorated with wreaths, ribbons, lanterns, and a life-sized manger in front of the pulpit. Straw was brimming from the four sides of the manger, wonderfully recreating the bed the Christ child must have lain on that cold winter night.

When my pastor stood to preach that morning, I sighed in relief. From the beginning of the service, I had already wept through several well-known Christmas carols. Each song reminded me of warm and wonderful memories from happier holidays. Each verse was pregnant with mental pictures of better Christmases past. So we moved from that emotional exhaustion into the message. I figured I could handle a talk much easier than a song. But something amazing was about to happen on that Sunday morning. The pastor began his sermon by reading a scripture:

> The Spirit of the Sovereign LORD is on me,
>   because the LORD has anointed me
>   to preach good news to the poor.
> He has sent me to bind up the brokenhearted,
>   to proclaim freedom for the captives
>   and release from darkness for the prisoners. (Isaiah 61:1, NIV)

"Is this year a difficult Christmas for you?" he asked. "Are you brokenhearted over a circumstance that has left you in great pain?"

Tears were streaming down my cheeks because I knew this was a message from God for me. All that moisture dripping onto my lap was silently answering his question: "Yes, yes, I am brokenhearted."

His voice mumbled on, but my mind remained on the scripture I had just heard: "He has sent me to bind up the brokenhearted." Once again tears streamed down my cheeks.

Meanwhile my pastor moved to the front of the pulpit and stood right beside the manger. He crouched down and said, "If you are in deep pain today, I invite you to leave your burden here in the manger. You don't need to physically get out of your seat and come down here. But in your heart, place all your brokenness on the straw of the manger. Remember, friend, Jesus Christ has come to mend that which is torn. He has come to bind up your broken heart."

I don't recall much of what happened after that except that in my soul I gave Christ the pain this crisis had created. It wasn't the sort of thing that was accompanied by harps, strings, or chills up the spine, but it was an awesome encounter for me.

Christmas became bearable, thanks to the One who had come to bind up my broken heart. God was loving me, healing me, and giving me strength.

As the New Year arrived, I tried to accept my new position in life and move on to the new dimensions awaiting me. Many positive things happened in that time period, but there were also moments of continued struggle.

I faced loneliness. I wasn't very comfortable with my singleness, and it seemed like every day there was some reminder of my life as a married person. I heard a song on the radio that used to be a favorite of my former wife. In a crowd of people, I would suddenly catch the scent of the perfume she had always worn. An item on a menu, a commercial on television, the slightest little thing could send me off into painful nostalgia.

Particularly painful for me was the sound of the alarm announcing a new day. As I rolled over, I remembered there was no one else in my bed to disturb. The other side of the bed was empty, and alongside it was a nightstand once brimming with books and tissues and magazines and knickknacks—now utterly naked.

The empty nightstand brought a lump to my throat at the start of every day. Its bareness silently testified to my pain. But God, the Great Healer, could bind my broken heart even in its daily despair.

After New Year's I was putting away the Christmas decorations. As I was about to box up the tiny Nativity scene that traditionally graced a table in the living room, a thought occurred to me. I decided not to place it in its box but instead give it a different year-round home. Carefully I moved the Nativity scene to a place where it could be loved and cherished—on top of the empty nightstand.

The night table was no longer a symbol of pain and loneliness. It became a place brimming with signs of renewal and hope. Every morning when I awoke, I rolled over and glanced across my bed to see the baby Jesus in His tiny manger. And I remembered He had come to bind up my broken heart.

My encounter with the Nativity scene occurred years ago, but the value of the lesson remains to this day, just as the magic of the moment did not end with the shepherds' visit to the Christ child. Luke records their reactions when they left: "The shepherds returned, glorifying and praising God for all the things they had heard and seen, which were just as they had been told" (Luke 2:20, NIV).

The shepherds didn't return home "having glorified and praised God," but rather they went back "glorifying and praising." That tense emphasizes continuous action. They kept doing it! They celebrated Christmas every day. I learned that I could take the healing and the wisdom of Christmas and use it all year long.

As you reflect on your life, are you in need of God the Great Healer? Are you like Sammy, needing to begin a relationship with the Lord Jesus? Since this issue is so crucial to our healing, we will talk about it more throughout the book. But now might be just the right time for you to ask

Him to be your personal Savior in the quietness of your mind. Trust Him with your life. You won't be disappointed, I promise. He will come into your life, and the process of healing will begin.

Maybe you already know the Lord but you are in a different place than you expected. Give thanks to Him for where you are. Glorify Him and praise Him. What He accomplished for us began in that manger and gives us power to live every day of the year that lies ahead.

3

I Need Help
from Others

DIVORCE IS OVERWHELMING. It feels like everything is ganging up against you.

Say that you're paying attention to what you are reading, and you decide to work on self-acceptance and healing from the Lord. Just when you think you are making progress in those areas, something unexpected hits your life. It can be anything from a crisis with one of your kids to a clogged bathtub. A painful conversation with your ex or a higher-than-anticipated credit-card bill. A low performance review at work or an attack by ten thousand ants in the laundry room. And because you are dealing with so much pain in the divorce proceedings, just the thought of more stress added to your life may seem like more than you can bear.

In the New Testament, the apostle Paul understood that concept. As if someone (could it have been a divorced person?) had come up to him and

7

said, "I am so burdened down. This is more than I can bear," he wrote these words to the church on their behalf: "Bear one another's burdens, and thereby fulfill the law of Christ.... So then, while we have opportunity, let us do good to all people, and especially to those who are of the household of the faith" (Galatians 6:2, 10).

I need help. Why are those three words so hard to utter? Does it make us feel worthless? (I feel like such a jerk since I can't solve my own problems.) Incompetent? (I'm so stupid. Everyone else knows what to do in this sort of situation.) Inadequate? (I don't even know where to begin to find the light at the end of the tunnel.) These are normal responses, but they are not right responses. We are filling our heads with a lot of negative self-talk if these reflect our conversations with ourselves.

God tells us over and over that we need others in our lives. That's just the way He wired us. It's not weakness; it's reality. We've bought into the superhero myth if we think we can solve any problem on our own without the help of anyone else. The next thing you know, we will start believing we can solve problems by ourselves in less than sixty minutes with a half-dozen commercial breaks!

I first realized I needed help as a divorced man when I sat down to assess my life up to that point. I made a startling discovery. In every phase of my life I needed help from others!

This is not a divorced-only club. No, I needed plenty of help from others when I was married. This is not an old-age issue. I needed help from others from my earliest memory as a child. It is not a cry of weakness, nor is it a mark of failure. We just need to understand and accept that if we are regular, garden-variety human beings trying to live in a way that pleases God, we are going to need assistance from other people.

Help!

Our world today seems to applaud the person who can go it alone. "I don't need anyone to help me" is the mantra of a new generation of isolationists. If we're not careful, we can fall into that trap and, in doing so, seriously damage our lives.

Lilly is a good example of what I am talking about. Brought up by a set of hardworking parents, Lilly learned early in life her parents' philosophy: "No one is going to help you out, Lilly. If you are going to be a success in this world, it will come from what you and you alone can do to make it happen."

So Lilly did her chores all by herself and got the extra baby-sitting jobs so she could earn a little more money for college. Mom and Dad told her early on that if she had any thoughts about education beyond high school, she'd have to pay for it herself.

A superachiever in school, Lilly won a variety of college scholarships and settled on a private college in the Midwest for her studies. Even with the full ride, she worked nights and weekends as a waitress in order to take care of incidentals not covered by the scholarships.

In her senior year at the university, she met Bradley. He had an amazing effect on her, because by her own admission, Lilly was an extreme introvert and a bit self-conscious socially. But Bradley swept her off her feet, and they were married a year later.

Lilly turned her degree into a wonderful career opportunity. She soon looked to be the woman who had it all: handsome husband, a couple of great kids, a successful career, the nicest house on the block.

Lilly was very happy. Bradley was not.

Feeling overworked and underappreciated, Bradley couldn't bring himself to confront Lilly, so he chose to act out in a passive-aggressive manner. He began an affair. It swept him up, and before either one of them knew it, the marriage was over.

"I was so devastated by my divorce, I didn't know what to do," Lilly now recollects. "But my parents had always taught me to be self-sufficient, so it never once occurred to me that I would need any assistance from anybody. I concluded that this was my lot in life so I better suck it up and move on from here."

As noble as that might sound, it didn't work. Lilly saw a pattern developing where devastation was followed by feeling overwhelmed. "I would snap back at my little ones when they asked me questions about their father. They were innocent questions, but I was so angry at him for leaving me with all this responsibility that I took it out on them.

"I would still be in big trouble if it hadn't been for Lauren. Out of the blue, she called me one day and invited me to lunch. As we caught up on old times, we realized it had been almost a year since we had seen each other. And in that time period, we both had divorced!

"As she shared her experience—she was about four months ahead of me in the journey—she kept referring to how others had been there to help her, to be a good listener, to be a shoulder to cry on, and even to fix the leaky roof in her townhome.

"It was at that point I realized I had *no one* to lean on. I had taken such pride in being self-sufficient that I hadn't built a circle of friends around me. No wonder I felt like I had no support—I didn't!"

Lilly thinks back to that lunch as a turning point in her life. Lauren convinced her of the importance of relationships, of friendship, and of getting help.

Help with the Kids

I realize not everyone reading these words is a single parent, but statistics tell me that quite a few of you, if not the majority, will fall into that category. Trying to raise children alone is a daunting task by itself. Add to it the whole process of trying to heal from a divorce, and it's clearly too much for one person to handle.

"I love my kids," Dan told me over lunch a few weeks ago. "And I'm glad the divorce papers gave us joint custody so we see one another almost all the time. I have the kids all week long, every week. Their mom gets them on the weekends. It's a good deal, I guess."

"It sounds as if there's a little hesitancy in your voice," I probed. "It sounds like you want to say, 'However...' Am I right, Dan?"

Dan looked at me as if I had just caught his hand in the cookie jar. "I'm embarrassed to say it, especially since my attorney worked so hard—at my demand—to get me custody of the kids, but...I just need a break now and then. With their being at the house every weeknight, by Wednesday or Thursday I do just about anything to have twenty minutes to myself." Dan looked horribly pained. "Am I a jerk of a father for feeling that way?"

"Not at all," I replied. "You are a wonderful dad. You're just expressing a natural desire for a little time off from the 24/7 responsibilities of parenting."

His reaction was one of deep relief. "Well that's good news," he said. "I was afraid you would think I was a bad dad."

"On the contrary," I answered. "I've been there; I know the feeling. So how can we get you a little well-deserved relief? And what would you do if you had a night off?"

"Well, there's this Bible study at the church on Wednesday nights that I would love to go to. I think that's part of why I have these feelings during the midweek. But how could I leave my kids? They're much too young to be left alone."

I responded with the most obvious answer. "Have you ever thought about a baby-sitter?" If you had seen Dan's face, you would have thought I'd just discovered a cure for cancer.

"Gee, I never thought of that. A baby-sitter is a great idea!"

I let him marvel at my superior intellectual capacity for as long as I could. Finally I asked him, "Dan, did you ever use baby-sitters when you were married?"

"Yeah, all the time," he replied.

"If it was a good thing when you were married, it might be a good idea when you're single."

He smiled and nodded. "It's amazing that I never thought of getting some help," he chuckled. "To make it even better, there are a couple of really wonderful teenagers in our neighborhood who are studying early childhood education in college. They have offered to baby-sit for free in order to see young kids up close and personal. So it wouldn't cost me anything to bring someone in every week."

Wow, that was simple.

But we're not thinking clearly when life feels as though it is unraveling before our very eyes. If you have struggles, you need people to help you. And don't feel embarrassed when they come up with a solution that is as plain as the nose on your face. At this point in life, you're not fully convinced you have a face, let alone a nose on it!

Transportation is another issue where help is definitely needed. I believe it is written somewhere in Genesis that as soon as humans discovered the wheel, they invented the carpool. Seriously, where would we be if we didn't have friends or neighbors to help us cart our kids around? Choir, soccer, gymnastics, youth group—multiply those activities by your number of kids, and the sum equals insanity! And I repeat my initial premise: I needed help with carpooling when I was a married parent, so why would I think I don't need help now that I am completely alone?

(As an aside, this might be a good place to insert a novel concept for your consideration. By their own admission, most families are overextended. Is it possible that this new season in your life could be the perfect time to simplify the schedule? Do you think your kids can survive with one extracurricular activity each? Trust me, they will still be emotionally healthy, well-balanced children even if they don't do sports and music and computer club and Future Farmers. I admit, it's not going to look as impressive on their applications to Harvard, but if you keep grinding away at your current pace, you'll never live to see them graduate from high school!)

I remember speaking at a single-parent conference sponsored by a local church that included a lively afternoon discussion group following my morning presentation. "What can your church do to lighten your parenting load?" a leader asked the group of moms and dads. A petite woman in her thirties stood and approached the microphone.

"My name is Barbara, and I've been divorced for three years," she whispered. "What I need most is someone to help me raise my two boys. I need men in the church to provide my sons with male influence and…"

The woman's voice was drowned out by applause. She waited for the cheering to subside, then continued her request.

"My boys need a man to play ball with them. They need someone to show them what a man's world is all about. They need someone to talk to about issues moms don't understand. They need a spiritual man who shows them how men walk with God."

As Barbara took her seat, other parents shot up to the mike and echoed her concerns. Most vented their frustration, but some offered success stories or gave suggestions.

Months after that conference I was still struck by the fervor with which these moms and dads talked about the need for mentors. Though I had been going through my own divorce issues at the time, my former wife was making herself available to our kids. Even though it wasn't as big an issue to me, I was seeing families who appeared to be abandoned by one parent. How could a single mom with boys or a single dad with girls raise them with no opposite-sex influence? Of all I heard the parents say that day, these three suggestions stayed with me:

Get on Your Knees

In our discussion group the afternoon of the conference, a woman named Saundra told her story. "For eleven months I prayed that God would bring someone to disciple my ten-year-old son, Jason. When I didn't find anyone right away, I assumed that God wasn't listening to my request. Then our pastor preached a message about prayer. It was just what I needed to hear. I resumed my daily request for a male discipler for Jason.

"One Sunday several months later a man asked me if there was anything he could do to help me. I was floored. I wanted to say yes right away, but I needed to ask a few people about this man. Eventually he began to disciple Jason, and my son is thrilled to have this gentleman in his life!"

Maybe you have prayed for months and feel as though God hasn't heard your request for a mentor. Or maybe you've given up on the idea, feeling as if the Lord will never send the right person. But, like Saundra, single parents must remember that God's timing is not our timing. Just when we think He's ignoring our prayers, He answers in unexpected ways.

Besides, in Psalm 68:5 He promised to be the father to the fatherless, and God does not renege on His Word.

Don't Expect One Person to Do It All

Even if God sent you the perfect mentor, he or she couldn't be all things to your child. You will probably find it necessary to seek out mentors who can mold your children in different ways.

For example, all children need spiritual mentoring. Though you are the most important spiritual guide for your child, look for men or women who fortify the foundation you have laid. A spiritual leader can be anyone from the youth group leader to the quiet woman who can be found praying on Sunday mornings in the back of the church. Once you spot such a person, approach him or her with your request to become your child's mentor.

Other areas where your children need mentors may include emotional, recreational, vocational, or physical (like a "big sister" with whom your teenage daughter can talk about puberty). When you spread the mentoring out in this way, it takes the burden off one person.

Look to the Church

Each Sunday look around for people who could be mentors for your child. Ask God to direct you to the right ones, but don't rule out any person. The man or woman you would least expect may have the most profound effect on your family.

In addition, ask your pastor to suggest ways that you can find mentors. Though some churches already have mentoring programs, many do not. Maybe God wants to use you to start such a ministry in your place of worship.

Make yourself available to others. If you're a single dad looking for a woman to mentor your daughter, offer to mentor a boy in the church as well. We often receive the biggest blessings when we are willing to reach out and serve others.

Help with the Mundane Routines of Life

Even if you're not a parent, you still need help. Most likely your divorce has attacked your regular schedule like a cancerous tumor. It's important to admit your need and reach out for help—even with basic stuff.

"I don't cook," Wyatt admitted. "I know that sounds old fashioned. I'm not a chauvinist; it's just not my area of expertise. I've always viewed time in a kitchen over a hot stove as a severe punishment for some heinous sin I committed as a young child. The sin was so vile that it remained unspoken in our family history, for I have no idea what it is.

"Consequently I have developed horrible eating habits since my divorce from Ellie. I grab fast-food takeout most nights on the way home from the office. My life consists of burgers, fries, pizza, and fried chicken. I've put on thirty pounds in the last year. I need a solution—and pronto."

Wyatt and I talked about everything from destructive behaviors to trans-fatty acids. Ultimately I said to him, "So, my brother, you've either got to learn to cook or bring in someone to cook for you."

A light came on over his head when I said the last part of that sentence. "You know it's funny you should say that, because I just met a girl in the break room at work who talked about looking for someone to help her change the oil in her car. She says she's not very mechanical when it comes to cars, so she wondered if I knew someone who could help her. As we talked, I discovered she is active in a singles group at a nearby church. She invited me to check it out."

"This is all really good information, Wyatt," I interrupted, "but how does this have anything to do with your need for better food?"

"She loves to cook," he replied, looking at me like I was an idiot for not figuring it out. "We laughed about 'trading' her cooking for an oil change. But now that we're talking about it, I think I'm going to take her up on it."

Sometimes it's just that easy. There is more to this story, but I'll save it for later.

HELP WITH BIGGER ISSUES

We need help with the mundane, but we also need help with the big stuff. God wired us in such a way that we help each other through our relationships. I'm not talking about dating here—we'll tackle that issue in a later chapter—but we all need the help Solomon speaks of in the Proverbs: "Iron sharpens iron, so one man sharpens another" (Proverbs 27:17).

Something wonderful happens when we can talk to friends about the hurt inside of us. They are able to pick up on blind spots in our lives. It never fails that when we talk to others, we come away with a better understanding of our situations. We don't always even need words back. Some of the best times are when we can talk and a friend will just listen. Even if answers aren't readily apparent, it helps to know that others will be there for us, as we want to be there for them.

Proverbs 27:17 is tucked away between two other strong comments about needing one another: "Oil and perfume make the heart glad, so a man's counsel is sweet to his friend.... As in water face reflects face, so the heart of man reflects man" (Proverbs 27:9, 19).

We help each other through a variety of issues. We help each other through loneliness. We help each other fight discouragement. We help each other stay on course.

"When my husband left, I thought I might as well curl up and die," Vanessa recalls of her divorce. "It was almost five years ago now, but I don't think I'll ever forget that feeling of helplessness and of being all alone.

"But thank God for Tina. I was overcome with dark, morose thoughts, and yet this angel from God came to my rescue by doing one important thing—she was my friend. She always had an uncanny sense of timing. It was as if God alerted her when I was particularly depressed. Somehow she would show up with a casserole or a new CD from a favorite singer of mine or any number of things just to let me know she cared and that I was important to her.

"One night in particular I didn't think I was going to make it. I couldn't stop crying. All I could think about was how much I loved my husband and how I couldn't live anymore if I couldn't be with him. I'm ashamed to admit that I was ready to take my life that night. I had a plan all worked out.

"I called Tina, and she instinctively picked up on my desperation. She was amazing. She kept me on her cell phone while she drove over to my place. She came to my front door, put her arms around me, gave me a big supportive hug, and stayed up with me all night talking through my anguish. The next morning when she was convinced I was okay, she left for work. I can't imagine how she worked a ten-hour day with no sleep, but she did. And as soon as work was over, she was back at my place to check on me. She is an amazing friend."

Help from Professionals

There is another layer of help that we need to delve into in greater detail. I am convinced that just about every one of us can use some professional counsel when sorting through divorce and the issues that led up to it. I have strong feelings about this topic, so I will address it more thoroughly in a subsequent chapter.

A Final Thought

One of the best ideas I have seen regarding helping one another came out of a divorce-recovery workshop sponsored by a local church. Understanding the need we have for assistance in various aspects of life, coupled with the biblical teaching that all of us are gifted by God, this group has come up with a team of workers they call their special task force.

The purpose of the task force is to link people's requests with those gifted to assist in that area. If your fence is falling down around your backyard, someone will show up to help fix it. And if you are gifted in bookkeeping, for example, you may be called upon to help a struggling young divorced woman file her tax return.

Not only does this get folks involved in helping other folks, but have you noticed there is no mention of money in these transactions? People volunteer their time and talents to make this task force work. Theologians would call this the body of Christ at work.

And where do you suppose this grand idea began? Remember Wyatt and Ellie, the oil changer and the cook? They were both so pleased with the outcome of helping one another that they approached the church leadership about starting this on a grander scale. Granted, paperwork is necessary to keep everyone's gifts and needs up to date, but, again, people in the church with administrative expertise volunteer to coordinate the calendar for the group.

You can do it with your group too. Whether from a special task force or a one-on-one encounter, we all need help. If you are currently hurting, reach out to someone who can help you. And when you are able, extend a helping hand to another brother or sister in need.

Part Two

Proven Helpers
Along the Way

4

The Advantage of Time, Distance, and Wise Counsel

SOMETHING NEW came into my life as a result of my divorce—tears. I can still recall trying to process all the events that were circling around me as life became a steady stream of new words: separation, attorneys, mediators, spousal support, child support, community property, custody. It was overwhelming, even if the rest of life was fine. But I was an emotional dishrag, and all I could think to do was sit down and cry.

I cried more in those six months than I had in the previous forty-one years combined. I remember crying so much that I would run out of tears. Have you ever had a "dry cry"? You are crying as you always do, but no water is present! That's someone who has really cried a river.

Hovering around my mind at the time of these tears was a constant thought: *It will never get better. It will be like this forever. Life will never be*

43

good again. I nearly had myself permanently convinced. Then one day I noticed a gradual improvement—ever so slight, but a tiny opening in the door to hope. What was the difference?

Time and distance.

Those are two very important issues in your healing. As the days, weeks, and months go by, you will begin to notice that things look clearer to you. By placing some distance between you and the crisis, you gain valuable perspective.

In the language of a psychologist, we are talking about the *process of grieving your loss.* Back in the 1960s, Dr. Elisabeth Kübler-Ross researched this issue in depth. Out of that study came the stages of grief, which pretty accurately chart the road most folks must travel after they have encountered a loss. Some lists are longer, some shorter, but the main elements are these:

- denial
- anger
- depression
- resolution/acceptance

Some lists add *sadness* and *bargaining,* but this group of four is essentially the list most professionals present. The process probably looks familiar to you. It is important to note that it is, in fact, a *process.* Except for the final point of resolution, these are not sequential steps. If you're like me, you find yourself revisiting stages of grief you thought you had worked through, but there they are again! Don't be afraid of grief. It is a normal part of life. Be kind to yourself; realize that since it is a process, grief is going to take time. You wouldn't break a leg and expect to be running a couple of weeks later. No, it takes time to heal. And so it is with grieving.

Our first response is to deny the catastrophe. Deep down we seem to believe that by denying it, we will make it go away. Unfortunately that is never the case.

I was pretty good at denial. I could even deny that I was in denial. My denial first manifested itself by my hiding. No one outside my immediate family knew of my pain. Part of that was embarrassment, but a large part of it was denial. "If I keep this quiet, everything will eventually come back together, and no one will need to know about the difficulties."

But the longer the trauma persisted, the closer I came to the truth. My marriage was over. I then began moving to the next stage: anger. I wasn't the type to shake my fist at God, blaming Him for all that was wrong with my world. But I *was* the type to get angry at my ex-wife. As I look back on what I said and did, I feel terrible about that time in our lives. Anger, though a necessary stage in grieving, is an ugly time slot.

I then headed along to the third stage: depression (while still bouncing back and forth through denial and anger as well!). I had heard a clinical definition of depression years ago, and now I was living it. Depression is anger turned inward. While I struggled with anger, I excelled at depression.

I was virtually useless as a human being. I sat around, moped, felt sorry for myself, cried, lost weight, couldn't sleep, became irritable, and only occasionally mustered enough strength to go outside to the garden and eat worms.

If it hadn't been for my friends, my counselor, and the Lord, I might not have made it.

As a child, I learned many rich verses in the Scriptures. Back then there was only one Bible to read—the *King James Version*. One of my favorite verses was tucked away in Psalm 46: "Be still, and know that I am God" (verse 10, KJV).

I've always liked that verse, but since my divorce crisis, I have come to love it. I tend to be a "churner," and the stillness that can only come from God is something I am learning more about every day.

By the way, now that I am grown up, I have gravitated to the *New American Standard* version of the Scriptures, which I discovered in seminary. The verse reads a little differently in that translation: "Cease striving and know that I am God."

The Lord must have known that I needed a crisis to bring me to a place where my striving would rise off the top of the chart. Through that rising I saw my overwhelming need for stillness. So after the crisis came the time and distance necessary to bring me to the place of peace and stillness that I live in today.

Friend, if you are in the thick of a crisis right now, it may look as if it will never get better. It may look as if it will only get worse. I have good news for you. It will get better. It may get worse before it gets better, but it will get better. It's just going to take time for you to heal and to create distance between you and this monster of a mess that has engulfed your life.

Seeking Help from a Professional

Speaking of this monster of a mess that has engulfed your life, it's important to consider another helpful suggestion. If you were driving in the desert and your car broke down, you'd gladly use your cell phone to call a mechanic. If you were in trouble with the Internal Revenue Service, you'd immediately call your accountant. If you were swimming in a pool of water thanks to a pipe that had burst in your home, you'd instantly call a plumber. The point is, when you are in a situation beyond your ability to handle, you call a professional.

It's the same with our lives. The mess that has been stirred up due to your divorce is potentially beyond your ability to decipher. Therefore, it makes great sense to consider seeing a counselor. Some of you read those words and have no problem with the concept. Others choke on the very idea of showing up for a counseling session. "I'm not sick! I'm no psycho! No one is going to institutionalize me!" Those sentiments may sound a bit rash to some, but others can relate.

I certainly do.

I went into counseling kicking and screaming. No, actually I went into counseling as a last resort because nothing else was working. After all, I had spent many years as a counselor myself; certainly I didn't need the kind of service I was offering others. Did I honestly believe I could heal myself? I attempted to pull the classic con on dear friends in order to get the name of a good referral in our area. I said, "I have a friend in my hometown who is having marital problems. Can you recommend a counselor for him?" I was as transparent as cellophane, but they played along with my charade and gave me the name of a counselor who helped me in tremendous ways.

Sitting in the waiting room at a counseling clinic felt like standing in a police lineup. I nervously went up to the receptionist's window, where I was forced to say my name aloud. No one waiting even bothered to look up, but I was mortified. I felt like saying, "Just hand me a sign to wear that says, 'I'm Bill Butterworth. I'm a very sick person, so you'll want to stay away from me.'"

Instead of a sign, the receptionist handed me a clipboard with an intake questionnaire to be filled out. I sat down in the sterile, all-white waiting room and felt my courage grow as I jotted down intimate details of my life—social security number, driver's license number, and a health insurance carrier.

But the last question squashed all intentions of bravery. "Why are you here?" was the query at the bottom of the page, with five or six lines of space provided. I nervously looked up at the others in the waiting room. They don't give a rip about me, I concluded. They probably feel just as I do and are looking for someplace they can hide.

I recall scribbling something incredibly unrevealing as my answer: "I am here to discuss some personal growth issues." That wasn't exactly a lie. Plus, I concluded that if I wrote down "My life is in the toilet," the counselor might institutionalize me on the spot.

I turned in the clipboard and bit my nails to the quick. It was fascinating how everyone waiting seemed incredibly gifted at avoiding any eye contact with the others.

Once I was ushered into my counselor's office, I chose to sit on the plain brown couch. I sat on one end, then took a tweed throw pillow from the couch and clutched it to my chest. This became my standard operating procedure throughout my counseling sessions. One doesn't need to be an expert in nonverbal communication to interpret the message of insecurity I was showing my counselor.

"So, what's on your mind?" he began.

His first words threw me. My mind raced. Inside my head I was screaming, "What? No small talk? No easing into this? What are you trying to do, cripple me mentally for life?" I felt as though I was living out a bad Woody Allen movie.

"What's on my mind?" I repeated in a vain attempt to stall for time. My mind wasn't cooperating.

"Yes, what brings you all the way down here to see me? If I'm not mistaken, your home is quite a drive from here. I would guess almost an hour away. Something must be troubling you. Can I be of help?"

This was the moment. I knew if I didn't shoot straight with him, I'd end up paying a lot of money for nothing. I needed him to pass just one simple test.

"Do you know who I am?" I asked. I knew I was far from a household name, but a lot of people knew me through my speaking and writing.

"Uh, no, all I know about you is what you wrote on the intake questionnaire, which wasn't a lot." He stared down at the form and gently shook his head. He seemed a little baffled by my question.

But I got the answer I wanted. I was absolutely anonymous. Feeling a blanket of protection because of my unknown identity, I opened up, and over the next few months this man heard about every hurt I had ever felt in life.

I honestly believe I learned things in counseling that I wouldn't have learned through any other means. Although I had ruthlessly held on to the prehistoric notion that counseling was only for psychos and the hopelessly neurotic, I am so thankful for what counseling helped me to do.

I learned to take responsibility for what was mine and not to take responsibility for what was not mine. A lot of what I was feeling centered on rejection. The thought of my wife's leaving made me feel as I had for much of my childhood, when I was the little fat kid who had no friends. Try as I might, I could only gain attention by performing humorous antics for my peers. And through these performances, I gained the acceptance I so desperately craved. But by the time I was an adolescent, I was plagued with the realization that, as the class clown, I was the life of every party, but I still couldn't get a date on a Saturday night, which is a serious form of rejection when you are a teenager.

This staggering fear of rejection led me to an overdependence on my marriage. In one particular session, my counselor asked what I would do if my wife left. I came unglued. It was the ultimate rejection, I concluded, complete with all its devastating pain.

This led to the realization that I believed I was a complete zero apart from my family. Since I had such little respect for myself, I desired the security of my family in an almost desperate way. Because of this desperation, my wife was feeling smothered. I was trying to do the right thing, but it was having the opposite effect. At one point my counselor said to me, "Bill, you are sucking the life out of her." Sure, she was making her own decisions, but there was a context to be considered.

Of course I had a lot of anger at this point as well. I was angry at the horrible situation in my life, but in reality I was angry at myself for being so paralyzed by the situation. I was unhappy with who I was, and that unhappiness, anger, and rejection were all intertwined in one large knot, most often found either in the pit of my stomach or squarely in the middle of my head.

I had to learn to deal with my faults in the breakdown of my marriage. It was easy to blame it all on someone else—easy, but not accurate. It was overly simplistic to say that my marriage ended for one reason. I had to own up to what I had contributed to its demise.

That wasn't easy for me, just as it isn't easy for me to write about it now. I have a history of looking for the easy way, as most of us do. I am thankful my counselor guided me through the more difficult pathway, and together we navigated it with an incredible amount of success.

I hope you find encouragement in my story. Perhaps it will give you "permission" to take that first step toward help. If you decide to visit a counselor, listing some expectations will help you choose one who is appropriate for your needs. For example, for me it was essential that the counselor be a Christian. I wanted to be assured that we held the same basic value structure so I would never be asked to violate my moral base. I have friends who have received wonderful help through non-Christian counselors, though I think that is a risky endeavor. I also have friends who had more extensive expectations of their counselors' qualifications. They needed reassurance of shared faith and also a clear understanding of their counselors' techniques and ways of integrating theology and psychology.

I understand that choosing a counselor is a personal thing. All I am asking is that you don't let anything get in your way of that pursuit. Perhaps speaking with your pastor is a good place to begin looking for a referral. Of course if you're going undercover as I did, be sure to polish up your "I have a friend who needs help" story. Maybe you can be a little braver than I was.

My counselor helped me see that I needed to make some changes in my life. I've devoted an entire chapter to the process of change later in the book, but for now, consider some of the changes that came about as a result of time, healing, and counseling.

Make Some Positive Changes

I am one of those people who thrive on schedules, routines, and traditions. While much about this personality type is commendable, it has an accompanying downside. My counselor helped me see that I was attempting to bury myself in busyness, never giving myself permission to enjoy downtime or take a break. My divorce had thrown me into an unhealthy routine that was horribly unbalanced. I became concerned about where this might be leading, so I began adding things to my schedule as a change of pace.

First of all I made *physical changes*. I feel better when I am taking good care of my body, and much of the benefit comes from varying my routine. I felt that this period of upheaval was an excellent time for a routine physical exam. My doctor strongly suggested I get more exercise, so I returned to taking walks just for fun. I wasn't walking to get anywhere. These were middle-of-the-day Saturday walks you wouldn't normally take. Being out of the ordinary is what gave it punch. I also began to play golf again. Participating in a sport you enjoy—whether it's tennis or jogging or hiking— is a wonderful diversion from all that's going on. Whatever it is, get the kids covered with your former spouse or with a friend. We all need a different setting in order to clear our heads.

I also started making *mental changes.* My mind was absorbed with so many things throughout the day that it was hard to take a mental break. But I found a couple of things that consistently worked for me. I loved to read, so I began picking up books again. First it was books that focused on recovering from divorce, but gradually I discovered the value of a broader range of topics. I discovered that a good mystery or suspense novel every now and then can do wonders. Being a full-time speaker, I am attracted to other communicators, so I returned to listening to others. I attended lectures at community centers, local churches, and anywhere they were speaking. I started listening to tapes of my favorite teachers or of those who were addressing a subject of particular interest to me. I discovered that in listening to a variety of women and men, I was presented with different approaches to life as they told their own stories. This was fascinating to me.

The list would not be complete without *spiritual changes.* I don't want to hurt anybody's feelings here, but I found that it was easy to get into a rut in my spiritual life. I went to the same church every Sunday, sat in the same seat, sang the same songs, and left at the same time. I needed newness in my spiritual routine. So I began attending a different church meeting. If your church is like mine, there are more activities each week than one person can attend. So I mixed it up. I went to the early service instead of the late one. I signed up for a men's weekend retreat that I had never attended. Granted, I was with a lot of the same people, hearing some of the same teachers, but something about a different time and a different place allowed God to speak to me in a new voice.

Enjoying nature is another way to make a spiritual change. I often forget the simple pleasures in relishing God's creation. I was locked up inside, so I opened the door! I went outside, took a deep breath, and looked around as far as I could see. It was wonderful. I did it more and more, and it was a good thing.

I know you're struggling right now. I know your feet feel like two-ton weights you can barely put in front of each other to walk. But in time, you'll be back at the top of your game. Even if all these ideas seem like wishful thinking to you, I encourage you to give them a try anyway. Take a look at children. When they come home from school and go outside to play, that activity seems to revitalize and energize them. It gives them what they need to return to the tasks of household chores and homework. Isn't it possible that the same change of pace can work for you?

The apostle Paul told the Ephesians to make "the most of your time, because the days are evil" (Ephesians 5:16).

Do you think he made this statement to encourage more busyness? Or is it possible that he had a change of pace in mind as well? You can make it happen in your life, and you need to. It boils down to an expression my kids used to say, and even my counselor said it to me. Listen to all of them, and heed their call…

Get a life.

5

The Value of Relationships

LIKE ANYONE ELSE, from the time I was a youngster, I have cherished the quality of friendship. Some of us like to have a handful of close friends; others of us look for just one special relationship. Either way, friendship is a jewel in life worth discovering.

It sounds so basic, so simple. Yet for many of us, friendship gets tangled up in our personal struggles. I wrestled with low self-esteem from my earliest memories, so I grew up thinking I needed to "win" friends. I made it completely conditional—"I'll do such and such for you if you'll be my best friend." It never dawned on me that someone would want to be my friend just because he liked hanging out with me.

YOU'VE GOT A FRIEND

I didn't like sitting around my house growing up, so I would visit the neighbors with kids my age. I guess I established those early friendships with an attitude of "Thanks for letting me hang out over here. This is way better than being at home." I went into these situations feeling like these little buddies did me a favor, which put them a notch above me. Friendship should be about equality, not one notch above another.

Fast-forward through high school to college. My friends tended to be my roommates in the college dorm. We had good relationships, but our relationships with one another were clearly secondary; we were more interested in girls. Therefore, investing time in a friendship with a guy was considered wasted time.

I met the girl who would become my wife during my senior year in college. Suddenly I had no need for anybody else in my life. She was my all. We were as close as two kids could be. We went to class together. We ate our meals together. We studied together. We did our laundry together. We were in love.

We married. Fifteen months later we had our first baby. Fourteen months after that we had another. Then a third. Then a fourth. Then a fifth. We had five children in ten years of marriage. Friendships? Who had time? And who needed them anyway? I had six "friends" right inside my house with my wife and five children.

But let's face it. When your kids are young, you really can't call them your friends if you are looking for an emotional equal. So that leaves your spouse. And friendship with your spouse is a good thing. A very good thing. However, we have learned a lesson, haven't we? If our spouses are our only friends, we have set ourselves up for a fall. For when your mate leaves, among all the other losses in your life, you have also lost your only friend.

That's how it felt to me. Sure, I had guys in my life but no friendship of depth. So I was middle aged, divorced, and alone.

The Rest of the Story

But this is a story of how God rescues us when we can't swim.

When my divorce occurred, I was heartsick, lonely, and discouraged, but most significantly I was *embarrassed.* I had an ongoing conversation with myself: "This can't be happening to me!"

"But it is."

"No. Other people get divorced but not me."

"It's happened."

"This is the kind of thing that happens to people who are mean and ugly and uncaring and sinful and inattentive and overworked and unbalanced and spiritually desolate and—"

"Stop it. It's happened to me. I'm no angel, but I'm no demon either. It's over. It happened to me. Now I need to pick up the pieces and move on with my life."

"I can't. It's just too humiliating. What will people think when they find out? I will become the laughingstock of my community. I can't deal with that possibility."

"What can be done?"

"Nothing. No, wait. I know. I'll hide. That's what I'll do. I will go undercover. No one is going to know I am divorced."

And with that pathetic self-dialogue, I set out to convince the world that nothing was different in my life. I was a happily married man—no troubles, no worries, no problems.

Of course the idea that I could hide something so major in my life is laughable as I look back on it. But while it was happening, I truly thought I could pull it off. Who blew my cover? My friends.

The miracle of this story is that even though I didn't spend much time investing in friendships, God put men in my life who determined to be my friend no matter how disinterested or distracted I appeared. They just showed up and continued their goal of loving me unconditionally. First it was Joe. Then it was Joe and Mike. Then they added Ron. And Ed. Soon Gary was in on it. Then Bob. Add Ken, another Ken, and Robert. Before I knew it, nine guys were regularly checking on me. Most of these guys did not live in my town, so checking required a lot of phone time, but those hours on the phone kept me sane when I was ready to do anything to dull the pain of my loss. The joke at the time was they feared I would get so depressed that I would attempt suicide by jumping off the roof of my house. But since I lived in a one-story dwelling, most of their concern subsided. After all, who was going to plunge twelve feet to his death?

Forgive me if that sounds a bit morbid, but it was exactly the kind of banter I needed from a friend at that time in my life. I was wallowing in self-pity. I was an island unto myself, convinced that no one else in the entire universe could comprehend the depth of pain and loss I was experiencing. No one was feeling it the way I was feeling it.

Ironically, none of these nine men had ever gone through a divorce. Looking back, I guess their role had less to do with empathy and more with simple friendship and unconditional love. These guys were putting flesh and bone on a proverb in the Old Testament. I had read it hundreds of times. Now I was starting to believe it: "A friend loves at all times" (Proverbs 17:17).

Why was I trying to hide from men who were genuinely concerned about me? If unconditional love truly means love without strings, then these guys would continue to love me even if I felt I had messed up my life.

As time passed and my healing continued, I realized how I cherished these guys for reaching out to me at such a difficult time. And I imagine plenty of other things were going on in their worlds that could have kept them from being there for me. But they chose to help a friend in need, and to this day I thank God for every one of them.

But I mentioned a key weakness in these relationships earlier in my story. Did you catch it? Most of them lived in another town. Truth be told, these nine men were from all over the country. Here I was ready to curl up and die in Northern California, and my friends lived in Southern California, Seattle, Phoenix, Colorado Springs, Omaha, Nashville, and even Boston!

There was a hole in my friendship balloon that was causing air to slowly leak out. I needed guys in my life who lived right where I live, who knew me in my everyday world—at the grocery store, the post office, the bank, the local church, and parent-teacher conferences with my kids. I needed someone to keep an eye on me and hold me accountable for my actions. Accountability. I needed it in a big way. I needed it as a married man, and I needed it as a single-again.

I was discovering a need that all of us have deep inside. The Lord created us as relational beings. We need each other. Among the myriad reasons that statement is true is the concept of holding one another accountable for our actions. I watch your back; you watch mine. You help me see blind spots I would miss otherwise. Your input in my life is not invasive but of great value. So what does accountability look like? It can unfold in many different ways, but consider a couple of examples.

The Importance of an Accountability Group

Carrie's divorce was the most devastating event of her life. She loved Kevin and had trusted him since their first date in high school twelve years ago.

To find out he had been carrying on multiple affairs during their ten-year marriage was the biggest shock Carrie had ever faced. Still, she wanted the marriage to survive. It was Kevin who decided it needed to end. He said his latest girlfriend was his soul mate, so Carrie would have to get along without him. She pleaded with him to stay; she knew they could work it out. But Kevin wouldn't hear of it; his mind was made up. Soon the papers were filed, and the marriage was dissolved.

Carrie's response was overwhelming grief. "I would cry for hours," she recalled. "Then I would just stare straight ahead into space. I had no idea what I was looking at." She tried her best to be a good mom to Mary and Michael, a couple of cute preschoolers left in Carrie's custody.

"Thank God for my women's group," she told me after a recent meeting where I was speaking. "I couldn't have done it without them."

"Tell me about it," I asked.

"Well, since you went through a divorce, you know what I'm talking about. In the early stages of divorce, you are like a walking zombie. You have no idea what you're doing. If it weren't for others in your life who can point out what is happening, you might *never* see it!"

"And that's the role your women's group played?" I asked.

"That and so much more. I had been in this group for years. Eight of us get together every Tuesday morning over coffee. We use a classroom in our local church, so we are able to have quiet and privacy. Most of us are the same age—now in our late twenties. But we have some gals in their thirties and forties as well. I like that we have women of various ages. The older ones in the group have been especially helpful to me. Originally the group was designed to study the Bible together, and we had a great time doing that. But it wasn't an official Bible study that followed a specific curriculum, so we started experiencing a change in our focus. In the last few years many of us have been going through tough times, so we began shifting to books that deal with pain and stuff like that. I was learning a lot, and then the divorce happened. Suddenly all this material I was learning was being put to practical use. I was hurting. All the other girls knew it. They were so helpful."

"In what ways?"

"The help went beyond the books we were reading. It was more about their *being there* for me. They helped in countless ways: baby-sitting, bringing meals, inviting me to join their family activities when Kevin had the kids—things like that. Before long, they grew into a group that held me accountable for my actions since I had no one else to look out for me. They would be sounding boards as I talked about struggles I had with Kevin or a problem that was developing with one of the children. We would discuss it and come to some sort of resolution, and they would support me by regularly asking how things were progressing. If I ever thought of doing something crazy, I would see their faces in my mind's eye. It kept me saner than I would have been otherwise."

"So you are a big believer in accountability groups?" I asked the obvious question.

"Yes, I am. Frankly, I don't know how people survive without them, especially those of us trying to process the pain of our divorces."

THE GUY'S VERSION OF ACCOUNTABILITY

My experience tells me that women are way more plugged into groups than men. We men are lone rangers, preferring solo work and foolishly choosing to go it alone. So for me to see the need for an accountability group in my life, it would take a catastrophe.

A divorce will cover that base.

Unlike Carrie, I did not have a group in place prior to my divorce. I actually thought I was to be commended for not needing other relationships outside my marriage. It took the end of my marriage for me to see what I was missing. But through my pain I was aware enough to realize I needed relationships. With guys that tends to mean early-morning meetings before the workday begins. Like six o'clock on Wednesdays.

Six o'clock Wednesday morning has meant different things to me throughout my life. My first teaching assignment was a class called New Testament Survey three mornings a week at seven o'clock, including Wednesdays, so six o'clock meant frantic preparation to be at least one hour ahead of my students.

When we moved to Southern California, I took a counseling position, which necessitated some six o'clock meetings. Then I pursued my speaking career, moved again, and have found myself seated on many Wednesday morning six o'clock flights.

But the best memory, the most cherished time of all, was when Wednesday morning at six meant I was able to meet with my accountability group. It began right after my divorce. One clear morning in May, I invited Alan to have a cup of coffee with me. "I am experiencing a void in my life," I admitted to my friend. "I don't have any men with whom I can be close. I need quality friendships, accountability, mental stimulation, and spiritual fellowship."

We put our heads together and invited three other guys from our church to join us. And, voilà, over a strong cup of coffee our six o'clock breakfast accountability group—Alan, Fred, George, Duwaine, and I— was born. Our group was quite diverse. We had guys who were divorced, married, and remarried. In addition to me, we had a business executive, an entrepreneur, a builder, and a math teacher. But we also had a lot in common. At the time we all had teenagers, attended the same church, and were about the same age.

These four guys became my best friends. We went to ball games together, and I finally had someone I could sit with at church each Sunday! They would call during the week to check in or to ask me to pray about something in their lives. But it's important to note that it didn't start out that way. It was risky to be so transparent at first. I didn't know these men that well when we began. But little by little we developed a special role in one another's lives.

The key purpose of the group was to provide accountability. As the months progressed, we became more open with each other and began sharing our concerns about our lives. If I told the group I had a difficult writing assignment that was giving me trouble, they would pray for me and even follow up with phone calls during the week to check on my progress. If I had a rough speaking schedule, they would call me—sometimes while I was on the road—to be certain all was going okay.

We talked about our personal lives, family situations, vocational issues, and spiritual struggles. We encouraged one another out of our similar needs and issues, based on answers we could discover in the Bible. We worked together at finding solutions and quickly agreed that God was the only one with all the answers. We held each other accountable to our word and to becoming the men God had called us to be.

If we weren't careful, the hour spent together could digress into conversations about sports, movies, or cars. So we started reading a book together, which kept us from breezing through the same routine each session. We searched for reading material that stretched us as members of our society, as fathers, as men, and as Christians.

One of the first books we read was Bob Buford's *Halftime,* a book deal-ing head-on with issues men like us were facing in midlife. We read one chapter a week and marked meaningful passages to be discussed each Wednesday. We took turns leading the discussion each week, and we weren't in a hurry to plow through the content, particularly if it struck a chord in the life of a group member. We were known to stay in a chapter for two months!

Everyone in the group understood that we could come into the meet-ing and say, "Guys, I have something important to share." This usually meant a particular need had surfaced during the week, and that's why we were together—to help each other get through stuff. When this occurred, the book would be put aside while five guys got on their knees and prayed.

Very early in the group's existence, one of our members had to deal with a serious situation. We all prayed for his circumstance, and we were thrilled to hear the next Wednesday that great progress had been made. We slapped him on the back and thanked God for answering our prayers. I realized from that incident that no one in the group was exempt from deep pain; we all had potentially devastating circumstances if we didn't fully sur-render them to the Lord. Because of one person's pain, we quickly achieved a level of intimacy that otherwise would have come only after reading a bunch of chapters.

If you aren't connected to a group like I just described, you need to get connected. I know it's hard to find one, so you may need to start one. Ask the Lord to guide you to the right people, and then open your eyes for indi-viduals to whom you can relate. I believe in this concept so strongly I rec-ommend that if you can't find a group to plug into and can't get a group going, you should consider asking a counselor if you could join a local group-therapy situation in order to meet the need.

There are no hard and fast rules for groups like these. I have a friend who has met with the same guys for more than twenty years! In my case, the five guys were a little bit more in flux. One dropped out, we added another, then another, then lost another. Consistency is important, but things happen to mix it up. Sometimes a new member was just what we needed to provide fresh input.

Then there was the day I announced that I was leaving the area and moving back to Southern California—my current home. I assumed the group was going to pack up and move with me and was shocked when no one offered (just kidding). I know guys don't cry, so I can't explain the watery substance present at our last meeting.

I don't believe there is a magical number for a group's size, although I would be more concerned about a group's getting too big rather than too small. Take my current situation as an example. These days I don't have an accountability group; instead, I have one guy who provides the same connection for me. We meet every week over lunch to discuss our lives in complete candor. His life is remarkably similar to mine, so we identify quickly with each other's issues. But guess what? He hasn't been divorced! Yet we still relate quite well. As you look to put people into your life, it isn't essential that they be clones of you. There will be differences, and that's okay.

The most important thing is that you get something going. You need people in your life—right now more than ever. Relationships are important to your emotional health and stability. Make some friends. Take a risk. Reach out. There may be some wackos along the way, but don't allow them to discourage you. Diversify. Cultivate friendships with men, women, married couples, singles, divorced; those who are younger, older, very much like you, very different from you. You will be the richer for it, trust me.

6

The Personal Power
of Forgiveness

OUR JOURNEY TOGETHER now brings us to the heart of the matter.

There is only one way to handle the ugly side of your past, and that is to tap into the personal power of forgiveness. Without question, this area is the key to your future happiness. If you get nothing else from this book, this is the chapter you need to read and reread until it permeates your heart. That's how important forgiveness is to you. So I apologize in advance if this chapter is a bit more pedantic than the others, but I have so much material I want you to understand. Think of it as going back to school, and this is your first class: Forgiveness 101.

"I hate my ex-wife; it's that simple," Perry said to me at an early-morning meeting. "For all the pain she inflicted in my life, I hope the rest of her life is lousy!"

I knew to tread gently, but I asked Perry to open up a little more about his situation.

"She ran off with my best friend," he continued. "Can you imagine? My wife is sleeping with the guy I grew up with, my roommate in college, the best man at our wedding. And she's doing it while I am home baby-sitting the three kids! I was so angry when I found out that I went down to the basement and put my fist through a piece of dry wall I had just hung during a remodel. My knuckles were bleeding, so I found a pillow, wrapped my fist in it, and beat the floor until pillow stuffing was flying everywhere."

I knew part of the answer for Perry's future was forgiveness, but I was timid to suggest it. After all, he might treat me like a piece of dry wall if I asked him to consider that he needed to forgive his former wife and his former best friend and himself. But it was what Perry needed to do. It's what I needed to do. And it's what you need to do.

Have you ever asked yourself, Why do I harbor such bitterness, such anger, such resentment, and a host of other bad feelings toward my former spouse? Most of us use that question to launch into a litany of our ex's sins, weaknesses, and character flaws. Although that is a normal reaction, I ask you to take a different tack. I am suggesting that it is in our best interest to get beyond those destructive feelings. The antidote to anger and resentment is forgiveness. The reason we are so bitter is because we haven't tapped into the personal power of forgiving others and asking them to forgive us.

"That's crazy!" you may reply.

But it's not. It's true. Let's break down some of the essential areas of forgiveness.

What If We Don't Forgive?

Perhaps you are thinking along one of these lines:

- This forgiveness stuff is not my bag.
- I don't want to go through the hassle of forgiving.
- My ex doesn't deserve it.
- I can do a lot of things, but don't ask me to forgive that so-and-so!
- What difference does it make anyway?

Again, all of those are normal and natural thoughts, but we need to change the way we view ourselves and our former spouses. To start, I can think of at least four results of not forgiving.

It Keeps Us Stuck in the Past

You are never going to get past the hurt and resentment that was created by the divorce if you don't do something to move forward. I am not asking you to rely on denial to get through your pain. I am asking you to process your pain and take steps to move ahead. But you really can't move forward until you make peace with your past—the key being forgiveness.

It Adds to Our Feelings of Isolation

When we harbor feelings of anger and hurt, we may fear reaching out to someone else. "I've already been burned once," we conclude. "So I've learned my lesson. I don't need anyone else in my life." This is natural but incorrect. We do need others. If we stay stuck because we haven't moved past our former spouses, we will end up hermits! Even Tom Hanks had Wilson in the movie *Cast Away*.

We Risk Emotional and Physical Damage

Isn't it ironic that we are concerned about the effects of a poor diet and lack of exercise, yet not forgiving those who have hurt us creates even more serious emotional and physical damage? One study suggests that harboring bitterness is more dangerous physically than smoking or obesity. Why would we know these facts and willingly ignore them?

It Gives Control to Those Who Hurt Us

Does the full power of those words register with you? By not forgiving your former spouse, you are giving him or her the power to control you! Who would want to give power to someone else in any circumstance? I want the control of my life in God's hands ultimately and, after that, in mine as much as possible.

WHAT FORGIVENESS ISN'T

It may be possible to get a better idea of what forgiveness is if we can get our arms around what forgiveness isn't. The forgiveness taught in the Bible may be different than some of your preconceived ideas.

It's Not Forgetting

When I forgive my former spouse, it does not mean I will automatically forget all the pain that resulted from our marital breakdown. That would be nice if it could happen, but it is simply unrealistic. We will still remember the pain and disappointment, but honest forgiveness can still take place nonetheless.

Forgiving is not forgetting; it is much bigger and better than forgetting. It's freeing!

It's Not a Feeling

As we will see shortly, the Scriptures command us to forgive. The Bible never commands us to generate feelings; biblical commands are based on acts of the will. I choose to forgive whether I feel like it or not. I may have a terrible time even looking those people straight in the eye, but I am still commanded by the Lord to forgive them.

It's Not Fair

You're right, forgiveness is not always fair. How can I simply say to my former partner, "I forgive you," in view of all the sleepless nights; all the physical, emotional, and mental abuse I endured; in view of the cheating, the lying, the complete disregard for my feelings? That doesn't sound very fair. And I agree. But to understand forgiveness from a biblical standpoint, we must use God as our model. It really wasn't fair that Jesus had to die on the cross for all that I did wrong, but He did.

It's Not Approval of the Offender

"I'm never going to forgive my ex-husband, because if I do, I will be saying to everyone, especially my children, that I approve of all the evil ways that accompanied him up to the end of our marriage," Pat said after hearing me speak on this subject. Many of us feel the same way, but it is vital to make a distinction between forgiveness and approval. They are two very different and separate elements. I can forgive my offender without condoning his or her behavior.

It's Not Easy

Forgiveness requires a certain degree of strength, discipline, and courage. It doesn't come quickly and effortlessly. Even though it is not easy, it is worth the effort. As you ponder the points of this chapter, consider all the advantages to forgiving. Many things in life of lasting value require hard work on our part.

It's Not as Hard as You May Think

Having just said forgiveness is not easy, it is important to follow up with a statement that will keep us from jumping to the opposite conclusion. Even though forgiveness requires effort, it may not be as difficult as you imagine. Take it from those of us who go before you. "I'm not forgiving her, and that's final!" some of us screamed defiantly. But eventually we came to realize that our lives are on hold when we stubbornly refuse to move ahead. That's where forgiveness comes to the forefront. I am willing to forgive in order to obey God, to do what's right, and to get on with my life. With that context, forgiveness really isn't as hard as you might think.

WHAT FORGIVENESS IS

Okay, now that we know what forgiveness isn't, let's see what forgiveness really looks like. What is forgiveness?

It's the Key

Without being overly dramatic or overstating the case, I can say that forgiveness is the key that unlocks the door to the rest of your life. Forgiveness frees you from your past so you may pursue the future. Think about the words of the apostle Paul: "Forgetting what lies behind and reaching forward to what lies ahead, I press on toward the goal for the prize of the upward call of God in Christ Jesus" (Philippians 3:13–14).

I want to move ahead with my life, but it's not going to happen until

I settle up the past. The key to settling up is forgiving all who have created damage in my life.

It's a Choice

You make the choice. No one puts a gun to your head and demands it. Forgiveness is not about conjuring up a warm, fuzzy feeling, either. You come to a place in your life where you choose to forgive. A cold, hard act of the will, volitional choice. Look at the act of forgiveness in the context of these verses:

> So, as those who have been chosen of God, holy and beloved,
> put on a heart of compassion, kindness, humility, gentleness and
> patience; bearing with one another, and forgiving each other, who-
> ever has a complaint against anyone; just as the Lord forgave you,
> so also should you. (Colossians 3:12–13)

Put your former spouse's name in those verses. Are you acting compassionately toward Barbara? Do you practice kindness toward George? Are you humble around Diane, or are you beating her down with your own stuff? Does Larry view you as gentle? Do you continue to practice patience with Matt? Are you bearing with Sally? Are you forgiving Dave?

It's Freeing You to Get On with Your Life

Peter puts it this way: "Casting all your anxiety on Him, because He cares for you" (1 Peter 5:7).

We have referred to this aspect several times already, so let me just review. You will never get on with the rest of your life in a rich, full, and satisfying manner until you take care of the past—forgiving your former spouse. If you choose not to, his or her ghost will haunt you well into the future and will possibly affect a new relationship that could blossom. Think about that. I don't know many people who would be in favor of that.

It's a Character Revealer

Allow the words of this Scripture passage to sink deeply into your heart: "Be kind to one another, tender-hearted, forgiving each other, just as God in Christ also has forgiven you" (Ephesians 4:32).

For some who read these words, forgiveness is the most difficult issue. But God may be using it to build stronger, deeper character in your life. Ted was as reluctant as they come to forgive his former spouse, but eventually he did. At a conversation over a cup of coffee, he reflected on a result he had not expected. "I guess the thing that caught me totally off guard was how my forgiving my ex made such a strong statement to my kids. Sometimes we convince ourselves that the kids really don't know what's going on, but they do! My son, who is fifteen, said to me, 'Dad, I know how Mom hurt you, and I've got to tell you, I am blown away that you could forgive her. At first I thought you were being a wimp, but by watching you, I think I get it. You've gotten past it and are moving on. I'm proud of you, Dad. Good job!'"

It's a Lifestyle

Forgiveness is more than a one-time experience. It is an ongoing process, literally without end. The disciples of Jesus tried to get Him to explain how forgiveness works, as described in Matthew's account. "Then Peter came and said to Him, 'Lord, how often shall my brother sin against me and I forgive him? Up to seven times?' Jesus said to him, 'I do not say to you, up to seven times, but up to seventy times seven'" (Matthew 18:21–22).

Now, before you do the math, let me explain that Jesus was not pitching an exact number but instead telling the disciples that forgiveness is a way of life. This tells me that there may be occasions in the future where I will once again need to forgive someone I have already forgiven. As long as there are people in my life, and people continue to sin, I will continue to need to practice forgiveness.

WHOM DO I FORGIVE?

I Forgive Me

One of the most famous verses regarding forgiveness is found in the little book of First John: "If we confess our sins, He is faithful and righteous to forgive us our sins and to cleanse us from all unrighteousness" (1 John 1:9).

God promises me personal forgiveness for all the things I have done wrong, and that includes my part in the destruction of my marriage. On the outside, people may see me as the innocent party or the real villain, but in God's eyes I am forgiven in either case if I confess my sin to Him and ask for His forgiveness. So if God forgives me, I need to get with the program and forgive me as well.

I Forgive My Former Spouse

Based on how we view the end of our marriages, we will hold either ourselves or our former spouses responsible. If we hold ourselves responsible, forgiving ourselves is a big issue. But if we hold our exes responsible, forgiving them becomes the biggie. But just as God forgives us, He also forgives our former partners. Therefore, we should do the same.

I Forgive Any Third Party Involved

More and more folks are dealing with a divorce that occurs with a third party's involvement. They are not exempt from our forgiveness. Just as God asks me to forgive myself and to forgive my former mate, He also wants me to forgive the other man or the other woman in the scenario.

I Forgive My Counselor

"I can't believe I spent all that money on counseling, and the stupid therapist couldn't save our marriage!" Kenny spewed out in exasperation. In a more lucid moment, Kenny may see that ultimately his counselor is not to blame for the divorce, but if he harbors feelings of anger and resentment toward his counselor, then he needs to forgive him.

I Forgive My Pastor

"Not only was my pastor no help in our marital problems, but once we got divorced, he suggested to me privately that I start attending another church!" Rachel was hurt, angry, and disappointed at her church's response to her divorce. The purpose of sharing that account is not to analyze whether the church was right or wrong in its response. The issue here is that Rachel has an opportunity to practice forgiveness in this context as well.

I Forgive My Doctor

"I blame my divorce on my doctor," Val reflects. "It turns out there was a lot going on with me medically that would have helped me understand why I was feeling the way I did. But during my routine exams, my doctor just moved on without clearly explaining what I was experiencing."

Here again, the issue is not if Val is right or wrong in her assessment.

But based on her view, she needs to forgive her doctor for his part in her life.

I Forgive My Aunt Melba for Setting Me Up

Forgiveness is not just about former spouses and third parties. No, it continues in our lives. Once we're healing and back on our feet, well-intentioned folks will see us as incomplete without someone else in our lives, so they will start setting us up with blind dates. This works out for some but is a disaster for others. I forgive you, Aunt Melba.

How Do I Forgive?

Based on all the information we have looked at in this chapter, we can boil down forgiveness into these four statements:

Forgiveness is an act of the will.

I understand that God forgives me.

Since I understand that God forgives me, I can forgive myself.

Since I understand that God forgives my ex, I can forgive him or her too.

Putting forgiveness into practice will involve personal effort in all four of these areas. First, you must make a choice. Will you decide to extend forgiveness as the Bible asks, or will you continue to stew in the juices of anger and resentment? The choice is yours, and it *is* a choice.

Second, are you clear on God's forgiveness toward you? He forgives all who confess their fault to Him, and "all" includes you.

Next, are you willing to accept God's forgiveness and extend it to yourself? God forgives you, so what keeps you from forgiving yourself?

The final step is extending forgiveness to your former spouse. The first three steps are personal and private, between you and God. But this step will require you to contact your ex in some way. Perhaps it will be in a face-to-face conversation or maybe over the phone. It could be that a hand-written note or letter is more appropriate, but whatever form your communication takes, make certain your message is communicated clearly. Be prepared for your former spouse to be less than receptive. He or she may not "get it." What's important is that the message is clearly stated and that you reap the benefit forgiveness brings.

Undoubtedly the first place to begin is with open, honest communication with the Lord. So let's take what we've learned in this chapter and frame it in the words of a prayer.

Dear Lord,

I come to You today, making a conscious choice. I am humbly admitting to You that I have done things wrong in my life. Right now I specifically confess to You the sins I committed that led to the end of my marriage. Thank You for forgiving me of my flaws. I pray You would make me a better person through the lessons I have learned in the last weeks and months.

So, Lord, if You forgive me, then I know I can forgive myself. Help me to feel the freedom that comes from moving on in my life. Remind me every day of Your grace, Your compassion, and Your mercy, and may I apply it to my life.

Lord, I need to go to my former spouse and ask for forgiveness and to forgive him/her. Give me the courage and the strength to do this. I know there's a good chance he/she won't even get what I am doing, but I want to be freed from the pain of my past and move on with my life. Help me to tap into some close friends who can support me in my intentions.

I love You, Lord. I can't fully understand why You would love me, but You do. With that love as my model, my standard, and my hope, I go forward in my life, basking in Your forgiveness.

Amen.

Part Three

Relational
Matters

7

From One Single Parent
to Another

I AM AWARE that everyone who reads a book on divorce recovery is not a single parent. I debated long and hard over whether to devote a chapter of this book specifically to the needs of parents. Ultimately I chose to include this chapter, fully understanding that some of you won't be in these circumstances. You have my permission to skip this chapter and move on to chapter 8. However, before you pat yourself on the back for moving a chapter ahead of the rest of the class, I invite you to peruse this chapter as a way to better understand what some of your brothers and sisters are dealing with. Your journey has its own set of twists and turns, but take a look at what others are facing along with the whole issue of divorce adjustment.

Working on this book has been a jarring reminder of all that transpired in my life more than ten years ago. So much healing has taken place since that time, but looking back over my writing, my notes, and my journals has brought it back to the forefront. Consider this little essay I wrote concerning life with my daughter and four sons, whose ages ranged from seventeen down to eight at the time.

My alarm shrieks a reminder of all that needs to be done before the kids leave for school. I wake the high schoolers first, then I begin an assembly line of brown-bag lunches lined up on the kitchen counter as I wait for the Starbucks to brew. About the time the pot's gushing sound signifies the cycle is complete, abuse begins.

"Peanut butter and jelly again?"

"Can't we have Twinkies instead of an apple just once?"

It's not fair to be subjected to this sort of mistreatment before caffeine is flowing through the body's system.

"Knock it off, you guys!" I bark back. "Everyone be quiet and eat your breakfast."

"You bought the gross cereal again, Dad. It tastes like tree bark."

I need their opinions of breakfast like I need even less sleep.

"We're out of here, Dad," they yell. One by one, loud voices depart, leaving me to the quiet of an empty house.

It's Wednesday—laundry day! Lugging my hamper filled with dirty clothes to the washing machine, I open the lid to discover someone left a load of wet T-shirts, briefs, and boxer shorts. I wonder how many hours the clothes have been there when I lift one musty shirt to my nose. Then I discover the dryer is also full. I carry the contents to one of my sons' bedrooms but quickly close the door on the catastrophic disaster I find there.

I walk back to the kitchen, where I pick up the cereal bowls left on the counter and head for the dishwasher. But it hasn't been run! "They can't pour a little detergent in a hole, close a door, and press a button?" I mutter to no one in particular.

I turn my attention to my stay-at-home job as a writer, and things are no better. Working at home has plenty of advantages, but when you're having a bad day at home, it has its drawbacks, too. I receive two phone calls back to back.

"We need the first eight chapters a week earlier than we anticipated," an apologetic editor explains.

This is followed by, "Your royalty check has been unavoidably delayed. I know you were expecting it by the first of the month, but I think, more realistically, you'd better plan on the first of *next* month. We're terribly sorry."

The stress is starting to get to me. My hands are misplaced on the keyboard of my laptop, so when I try to write "I'm having a bad day," it ends up "u;m gacubf a vas sat."

By late afternoon, I drag myself back to the kitchen thinking it will divert my attention from work, turning instead to preparing dinner. You know you're having a bad day when this chore rises to be the day's high point. I decide that spaghetti is the way to go. Meanwhile, the gang is returning from school.

"I told Nathan's mom that you'd feed us dinner. Nathan hates spaghetti!"

And another of my favorite scenarios: "Don't make dinner for me, Dad. I had tacos and french fries on the way home."

By now I have scooped the spaghetti onto the plates and topped it with sauce from a microwaved jar. My glasses steam up from the rising heat as one by one each child grabs his plate, takes it into the dining room, and scarfs down the food. This is against the rules since I like to eat *with* my family, not *after* them. It is not to be on this particular evening, however, for when I reach the table, I am dining alone.

Perhaps it is better that I am left to myself. I determine that things will be different tomorrow. With my notebook placed to the right of my plate, I busily map out a strategy for changing things around here. A pile of laundry left unattended or one load of dirty dishes throws off the entire system.

I put the finishing touches on the chore chart I develop for the rest of the week, including letting John pack the lunches, Jeffrey fold the clothes, and each child devote forty-five minutes a night to individual room detail. Most of all, however, I remember what most easily falls by the wayside in busy times like these—my quiet time with the Lord. I remind myself it is as important to the kids as it is to me.

We gather before we go to bed. I remind the clan that it takes all of us to make this family work. Then I share a scripture and offer a prayer. I ask God to forgive me for not putting Him first today. I tell Him I need wisdom for everyday living and strength to go on.

I help the younger ones get ready for bed, tuck everyone in, turn out the lights, and stumble wearily back to my own bedroom. As I pull back the covers, a small piece of paper on the pillow catches my eye. My eyes fill with tears as I read a note from my daughter:

Dear Dad:

Thank you for everything you do for the boys and me. I know we don't express it enough, but we sure do realize it. Thanks, Dad. I love you!!

I crawl into bed and spend a little more time with God. As I turn out the light, I thank Him for each and every one of my precious children. And

I thank Him for helping me discover that the best cure for a bad day is a good night.

Cuts and Bruises for Kids of Divorce

In a perfect world, children could skip through life like skipping through the park. They are young, innocent, and carefree. Consequently, the walk is devoid of pain. It's as perfect as one can imagine.

But in reality, a skip through the park can be a trip fraught with pain. Who hasn't watched a child fall on the concrete and skin a knee? Or take a tumble off the monkey bars? How about the dear little one who bends over to smell the rose, only to be pierced by a thorn while trying to pick it up?

Life is like that skip through the park. There are fun moments—wonderful, memory-making, fun moments. But they are often interspersed with steps of pain. Our kids know the fun of life, and they know the pain. Right now, it may seem that most of the pain comes from the divorce. And as a result, our children may bring a new set of beliefs or a new form of behavior to our lives.

So what cuts and bruises are our children dealing with that are specifically related to our divorces? Here are a few for your consideration:

Kids Can Believe the Divorce Was All Their Fault

In most of our situations, this is utter nonsense. It really wasn't about the kids, but for some unexplainable reason, most kids go through a season in which they conclude the divorce would not have occurred if they had obeyed more, kept their rooms cleaner, made better grades, or fought less with their little brother.

If a child feels responsible for the divorce of his or her parents, this can increase the child's anxiety. If the anxiety goes unchecked, the next step is reactivity, where the child picks fights with everyone around. Left to itself, this will lead to polarity, where the child is as far away from his mom and dad as he can be. Of course the answer to this downward spiral is to catch it at its start, which isn't always easy.

A counselor once told me that a good rule of thumb is to expect a child to handle the divorce about as well as the parents handle it. That's why parents who seem to move through their divorce more smoothly have kids who seem to do the same. Likewise, the parent who is in a puddle probably has kids in the same pool of muddy water.

So how do we treat this bruise? Give your children large doses of *love* and *support*. Reassure them in no uncertain terms that the divorce was not their fault, and then back it up with extra hugs, squeezes, and kisses. Don't clock out of their lives. Be there for their soccer games, their school pageants, and the Christmas play at church. Leave them little love notes on their pillow, or if they're not in your home, send them notes in the mail. When I packed my kid's brown-bag lunches, I used to write a note on the napkin I placed in the bag. Of course, they ultimately got to the age where they had to sit me down and kindly tell me that they were becoming the laugh of the high school cafeteria, but at least they knew my heart.

Kids Can Regularly Test Your Limits

A second bruise our kids may bear—testing our limits—affects their behavior. Naturally this is true in two-parent homes as well, but limit testing can be especially stressful for a single mom or dad. If we're not watching them and ourselves, we can be guilty of contributing to this pain.

Don't treat your child like a parent is a good rule to observe. Without realizing it, we can realign the family structure to where one of our kids takes the role of the missing parent in the home. I unwittingly threw my daughter into lots of "mother activities" in my effort to raise her and my four sons. With her being the oldest child, it seemed to evolve naturally. But looking back, I realize it wasn't healthy. I robbed my daughter of some of her childhood opportunities.

Don't use your child as a messenger is another bad habit to watch for. We'll discuss this in greater detail in the next chapter, but for now suffice it to say that we send our kids on a trip they don't want to take when we force them into being middlemen or, even worse, spies. "What's your mother doing?" may sound like an innocent question, but it's not. First of all, it's none of your business what she is doing. Second, it places your children in an awkward position. They may know that the answer will hurt your feelings, so they must decide whether to tell you and hurt you or lie to you. What kind of place is that for a child to be in? And put there by us!

Of course, you should *never speak negatively of the other parent.* I know you will be tempted to violate this principle regularly, but you must discipline yourself to refuse the urge. Speaking badly of someone benefits no one. The very best thing you can do is to concentrate on your former spouse's strengths and consistently make them known to your kids. You may not see the value in doing this right now, but trust me, these kind words will come back to benefit you, just as harsh words will come back to bite you. So be positive.

Don't let your children manipulate you is a big rule at this point. Their regular testing of your limits will include pushing every button they know how to push in order to get what they want. If you see your little ten-year-old sad and despondent over life's circumstances, try to ascertain if it's genuine. Many a kid has scored a shiny new bike as a result of manipulating the parent!

The answer to all of these issues is to *give your child the gift of firmness*. As difficult as it may be for you, particularly at this time, your kids don't need a complete softy. They need you as well rounded as you can be, loving and firm in the rules.

Kids May Misbehave

As with testing your limits, remember that all kids misbehave, no matter what their family situation is. But it is vital for single parents to try to determine if the misbehavior is related to the divorce or just normal for a child that age.

Think about the extra burden our children are carrying. I read recently of a course offered at a local junior high school entitled "Who Gets Me for Christmas?" Among the many topics covered in the course were "Tug of War," "Nothing's Too Good for My Child," and "You Spy!"

A counselor can be very helpful in clarifying what we parents cannot see. I recall spending an entire session with my counselor on the topic "Is this particular child of mine acting in certain ways because his mom and dad divorced, or is he just acting this way because he is a teenager?" One hour later his answer was an emphatic yes!

The counselor explained how much I love for all issues to be black or white. "Bill, you want this question answered by me saying, 'This situation is all about the divorce' or 'This situation is just normal adolescent behavior.' Sometimes it can't be distinguished. In this case, your son is demonstrating behavior that most likely reflects both typical teenage feelings and some stuff resulting from the divorce. I know you don't like answers like that, but it's the truth."

The best answer for misbehavior is to give your child *consistency.* Remember how you handled your child prior to your divorce? Was he wild, crazy, and out of control back then? Or was he more calm and obedient? If the former, you need to check out material on raising good kids. The literature will tell you it's all about consistency. Make rules and abide by them. If you think you're being loving by letting your kids get away with something, you've got it wrong. They may look appreciative at the moment, but deep inside they are hurt that you don't care enough for them to stick to your guns.

But many of you remember how good your child was prior to the divorce. Chances are you were doing a better job of being kind, consistent, and loving. As difficult as it is, it's time to return to those days of parenting when you were more focused on them and their needs.

Be realistic. Consistency was tough when life was better, so it's going to be even tougher with the circumstances surrounding you now. Give yourself a little slack, but not too much, for your children's future could well hang in the balance. It's a tough tightrope to walk, isn't it? You need to give attention to your healing, but you need to be actively involved in your kids' lives as well.

Kids Can Fluctuate All over the Emotional Chart

It was true prior to the divorce, and it's just as true now. Well do I remember the season my daughter entered adolescence or, as I chose to name it, "add less sense." Emotions I had never seen before in her life reared their ugly heads. Don't get me wrong. She wasn't misbehaving or embarrassing me in public or throwing plates across the room, but she was behaving differently than I had previously experienced. Later I would learn that it was the natural result of hormones and their friends, but it threw a major curve ball in my life. I thought I knew my daughter, but I had never seen this behavior. The biggest telltale sign was wrapped up in one sentence: "Daddy,

I'm crying, and I don't know why!" Of course, I didn't know why either, so I wasn't much help at the time. But I tried to be supportive even though this was new turf for me, too.

The answer to children's fluctuations is to *give them stability.* It may be normal and natural for them to be happy one minute, sad the next, then angry, sad, glad, or afraid. Encourage them to express their emotions, but it works best in the context of your personal stability. If their sadness makes you sad, they won't feel as free to share the next time. They will feign happiness in order to cheer you up.

Here are some practical suggestions for maintaining stability with your kids. *Establish and follow a routine.* Following a schedule sounds restrictive to some, but it provides just the opposite effect—it frees everyone up! Knowing what is happening at what time and who is responsible for what task can unlock the door to harmonious family life.

Celebrate special days. This is obvious for birthdays, Christmas, Easter, Halloween, and Valentine's Day, but consider broadening the celebration base. How about the first day of school? the last day of school? the completion of a term paper? the end of Little League season? report cards? The list is endless, based on your creativity and imagination.

I know what you're thinking: celebrating is expensive. It can be, but it doesn't have to be. You can pull out all the stops occasionally for a ripsnorting party, but you can also get out the markers, construction paper, and crepe paper to make posters and banners that more personally celebrate the "I finished my book report on *The Great Gatsby*" party.

Regularly affirm your child's worth. We all know the pain of self-rejection. Remember chapter 1? If you and I are dealing with self-esteem issues as adults, imagine what our children are wrestling with! Don't just affirm their accomplishments, but give them hugs and attaboys just for being who they are. If we only reward what they do, they'll conclude (correctly I might add) that we only love and accept them when they perform. We're going for unconditional love here.

Maintain boundaries. As much as I am tempted to pull my world in around me, drawing a tight circle around my children and myself, doing so will damage them and me. I must intentionally pursue my own life. There are places and times that are for me alone, without the children, just as there are times and places for my kids without their dad. It's not a bad thing. On the contrary, it's healthy. We need our separate lives as well as our lives together. Setting up strong boundaries allows each of us to maintain a healthy, unique identity without being overly dependent on someone else.

This is a crucial point, because some of us didn't have healthy boundaries with our mates, and consequently the divorce was even more devastating than normal. Now is an excellent time to learn the benefits of boundaries and apply them aggressively to your life. My friends John Townsend and Henry Cloud have authored numerous books on this issue. If you haven't already read one of their books, pick one up.

In my early days of single parenting, I heard a speaker address single parents. I'll never forget the encouragement he gave us. He told us that this season in our lives can be a time of four things:

- A time of strong bonds
- A time of strong children
- A time of strong lessons
- A time of strong faith

He was right. All four of those issues came to light during my years as a single dad. We grew closer as a family; I could feel it. My children grew in ways I could have never imagined. To say I am immensely proud of my five grown kids is an understatement. We all tried to learn the lessons God had for us. Some of us learned more quickly than others, but we learned. Some of us have learned more than others, but we all have learned. And our faith grew as a result. When everyone else in life disappoints you, God remains faithful. He is the One to whom we look. He is the Perfect Parent.

He will never disappoint. Remember His promise in Psalms:

Sing to God, sing praises to His name;…
A father of the fatherless and a judge for the widows,
Is God in His holy habitation.
God makes a home for the lonely. (68:4–6)

8

The Ex Factor: Getting Along with Your Former Spouse

ONE OF THE MOST difficult aspects of a divorce is dealing with the former spouse. And this difficulty only intensifies when children are involved. Many of us would feel more comfortable never seeing our former mates again, but this isn't possible when there are kids. This can be a real test of our faith, so I thought it might be helpful to share a few ideas I have gleaned from talking with many divorced men and women over the years.

In some respects I consider myself an expert in dealing with a former spouse, if you qualify for expert status by making every mistake known to man. In my early days of dealing with my divorce, I was a sad case indeed.

I went through a phase where I was one angry dude. I got to the point that I couldn't speak to my former wife in a subdued, calm voice. Even when we spoke on the phone, I lashed out in angry rampages about how I viewed the state of our dissolution. Sometimes I hung up the phone with such force I fully expected the receiver to shatter.

Of course, there were other phases. The anger could be replaced with the sad, desperate pleas of a shattered man. "Won't you please consider getting back together? We can make it work this time; I just know we can." Pleading would lead to begging, and begging would lead to the total loss of self-dignity.

The zombie mode was another interesting facet of dealing with my ex. I would see her in order to take care of a business matter or pick up or drop off the kids, and I would exhibit nothing more than a blank stare. "Are you okay?" she would ask.

"Whatever," I would reply with all the feeling of bituminous coal. Blink and stare, blink and stare—a very unhealthy, nonwinsome pattern of behavior.

Add cynicism, disrespect, and other ungodly behavior, and you could pretty much fill out the package known as Bill Butterworth in my early days of divorce. It should come as no surprise that my former spouse was far from responsive during this time.

However, I have good news. Enough time has gone by, and enough lessons have been learned by the man who could do nothing right, that my former spouse and I are actually getting along quite well these days.

Discussing former mates cuts a broad swath across our country. Some divorced couples live half a continent away from each other, and others live right down the street. For some, the divorce is so fresh that dealing with the ex-spouse is about the most painful experience imaginable. Others have been on their own for a while, and the degree of difficulty has lessened over time. Some folks still feel connected because of elaborate financial contracts, while others feel completely on their own, because all issues, including financial ones, are finished. Talking about a former spouse is indeed a challenge. My hope is that perhaps some of these issues will ring true for you. Consider a few "I wills" and "I will nots."

I Will Establish Healthy Boundaries

You're not married to this person anymore. I know that's basic, but you may want to write it down on an index card and put on the front of the refrigerator with your favorite magnet.

Since you're not married to this person anymore, you are not responsible for his or her behavior. You don't need to fix her flat tire if that's the only reason she's called you in the last ten weeks. You don't need to send him frozen casseroles with the kids because you know when he's by himself he eats nothing but junk. You're single again, dear friend. And part of what that means is that she will ultimately have to learn how to take care of herself in automotive emergencies. And he will either start eating healthier or face the consequences at his next doctor's appointment.

It's not your fault in either case.

Frankly, both of those illustrations can be modified as time goes on and you establish your own boundaries. It could be a nice gesture to help with the car or to send a little dish of goodies. But if you feel it's your *responsibility* to perform those tasks, we need to address the motive.

Part of the reason for some divorces is that the wife mothered her husband or he acted more like a daddy than a mate. These are complex issues that may require a competent counselor to work through. For now, you've got enough on your plate just trying to make sense of your life, beyond waiting by the phone for that phantom call that asks for your help. You're divorced now. You have to give it up. It's not about "us" anymore. These days it's more important to think about you.

A few weeks ago I ran into an old friend who provided the perfect illustration for what I am saying.

"I must apologize for yawning while you're talking," Brandi said to me at a recent social gathering. "I didn't get much sleep last night, and now I am paying for it."

"Is everything okay?" I asked gently.

"Yeah, I guess." She sounded reluctant. "I did a stupid thing last night."

"What happened?"

"Keith called around ten last night to say he was stuck at a meeting and needed me to go over to his house and check on the kids. It was his night of the week to have them. They were with a church youth group until ten, and then they would be heading home to an empty house. So I agreed to go over there and watch them until he arrived."

"When did he get home?" I asked, fearing the worst.

"That's the problem. He said he would be home by eleven, so could I make sure the kids went to bed and just wait around. I did what he told me, except he didn't get home at eleven. He pulled up the driveway at one thirty! He kept calling every half hour, saying it would be just a few more minutes, and I believed him! It's just like it was in our marriage, only worse. I should have taken the kids home with me at ten. I knew it, but I didn't act on it."

Do you see the control Keith still wields in Brandi's life? She has to get to the point where she does not allow him to make demands on her schedule. It's complicated because of the children, but there are ways to establish healthy boundaries that make the point yet do not penalize the children.

I WILL NOT USE THE CHILDREN AS GO-BETWEENS

When I first met Rick at a divorce-recovery workshop where I was speaking, I could tell by the dark circles under his eyes that he had traveled down a rough road. After my session, he came up to discuss a couple of points I had made in my presentation. As I invited him to share, he opened up more about the pain he had experienced in his divorce that was not quite a year old. The more he talked, the more his former wife sounded like a source of intense pain and tension in his life.

"It sounds like things are okay between you and your two daughters. How are you dealing with their mom?" I asked after he had told me his story.

"Well, that's a positive part of my story," he announced with a sigh and a big smile on his face.

"You two are getting along better?"

"No, not really," was his honest reply. "I have decided that everything I need to handle with her I will pass on through my kids."

"Your kids?"

"Yeah, that way there's a lot less hassle. She won't give our daughters the hard time she would have given me."

Rick sounded so pleased with his system for alleviating stress. It was difficult for me to critique his method, but I felt I had to, if for no other reason than for the sake of his children.

"Rick," I began, "putting your children in the middle may lessen your stress, but think what it is doing to your girls. They're being put in a role that must cause all sorts of extra worry for them. They don't want to hurt your feelings, and they don't want to hurt their mother either."

"I guess I never thought about it from that angle," he admitted. "I thought I was doing them a favor by avoiding arguments with their mom."

Most of us fall into the same pattern. We don't *intentionally* put our kids in the middle of something, but nonetheless it occurs. Perhaps one of the best solutions is to have a serious talk with your kids. Ask them if they feel they are being put in the middle of something. Just one word of caution: be prepared for an answer you may not expect.

I Will Not Use the Children as Spies

One step beyond go-betweens is the tendency to use our kids as spies. Maybe we're so new at it that we come right out and ask the kids, "So, tell me all about your father's new girlfriend!" Or perhaps we've matured in our single-parenting process so that we ask questions that are less blunt but are open ended enough to get the children to talk. You know how it goes:

"Did you have a nice weekend?"

"Yeah, Friday night we all went to a movie."

"Oh…who all went?"

"Just us kids and Dad and his date."

"A date… That sounds fun… Was she nice?"

Before you know it, you've put your kids in a situation where they've described Dad's date from the top of her blond hair (did it look real or dyed?) down to the size shoe she was wearing, the seating arrangement in the movie theater, and a promise from the kids to get her tax records from the last five years on your desk by next Monday morning.

This is a tough principle to master, I admit. Our human nature has a morbid curiosity about things of this nature. But we're all in a much better place when we resist the temptation to pry and instead move on with our lives. You'll be better off, and your kids will most certainly be relieved to avoid another uncomfortable situation.

I Will Do My Best to Get On with My Life

For me, part of the deepest pain about being single again was that I didn't want to be single. I liked being married. I liked having someone to come home to. I didn't want to deal with myself as an individual. I wanted to be in a relationship.

So when my marriage ended, I had a difficult time letting it go. I hung on to the pipe dream that my storybook life was going to return.

It didn't.

One of the best pieces of advice I ever received was from a friend who loved me enough to talk straight to me. "Bill," he said, "you've got to get on with your life. Stop living each day like you're a giant Hold button on a telephone. There's no reason to drag your feet. It's time to get on with what you want to do with your kids and your career and *you*."

I appreciated the advice but didn't necessarily want to hear it at the time. I wanted my wife back, though it wasn't meant to be. All the wishing and hoping weren't going to make any difference.

I learned to set some goals, pursue some quests, and dream some brand-new dreams. Much is accomplished by doing that, not the least of which was getting along better with my former wife.

I Will Honor the Financial Arrangements

This is the touchiest issue, bar none. So much could be said here, but let me boil the issue down to its most basic elements. All the counsel I have received on this topic I can sum up in two sentences:

1. If you are the person responsible for paying spousal support and/or child support, honor your agreement. Pay the full amount, and pay on time.

2. If you are the person who receives spousal support and/or child support, honor your agreement. Don't continually nag, whine, or renegotiate for more money.

The most common complaint comes from the person who is supposed to receive support but doesn't get it. What should she or he do? I would begin by suggesting what *not* to do, and that is whine, nag, and complain. Your ex is not going to feel more motivated to write the check because of that behavior. Instead, contact your attorney and/or the legal authorities. If your former spouse is violating his or her legal contract regarding support, it needs to be addressed with all the authority of the law. I know that sounds harsh, but if you have calmly and quietly confronted your ex with the issue and there has been no response, you have no other alternative.

I'm sure there are exceptions to both of these, but just for fun, try living by these rules for the next six months. The outcome may surprise you.

"How's life treating you?" I asked Adrian one morning over coffee.

"Actually, quite well," he responded with a tone in his voice that made it sound as if even he was surprised at his reply.

"Why so chipper?" I prodded.

"Well, I've made some adjustments to my schedule, and in doing so, I've stumbled onto something that has lifted a huge burden off my back."

"Tell me more," I urged.

"Well, as you know, it's been a little over a year since Gina and I split up. And I have to say, I've been growing and maturing a great deal throughout the entire ordeal."

"Yes, I've seen it," I encouraged my friend. "And I am very proud of you."

"Thanks. But one particular aspect of the divorce has stuck inside me like a little seed that becomes lodged between a couple of teeth—the financial side of things. I admit, the first of the month has been the most depressing day on my calendar. Writing that spousal support check to Gina just eats away at me. To be honest, it became such a sickening thought I actually began delaying the payment. Gina had to call me three months in a row to ask if she would be getting the check anytime soon." Adrian fidgeted nervously in his chair, obviously reliving the pain of what those phone calls must have been like.

"I determined it was my duty, based on the judge's decision, to pay her that money every month, so I was going to do it and do it in a timely manner. As a result, I now write her a check for the next month on the twentieth of this month. She gets her check ten days early!"

"And it's obviously working out?" I asked the leading question.

"It's great! She's not hassling me with phone calls, and I'm not leaving her hanging out to dry trying to figure out if and when she'll get the check. It feels good doing the right thing."

Yes it does. It feels good doing the right thing.

I Will Practice Forgiveness

Forgiveness is the heart of the matter. The value of this attribute was discussed in greater detail in chapter 6, but this is an appropriate place for a review. When divorced people can forgive their former mates for the dishonoring treatment of the past and can ask for forgiveness for the anguish they also brought to the marriage, a great step is taken.

"I can forgive anybody else on this planet. Just don't ask me to forgive Brandon," Peggy said to me not long ago. "What he did to me and what he did to my children took him over the limit in my book. Forgiveness will never happen."

I understand Peggy's position. Many of us have been in a similar situation at one time or another. I had a hard time generating the energy for forgiveness. It wasn't until someone shared with me an important concept: *without forgiveness, the other person still exercises a degree of control over you.* We all want to get on with our lives, get out from under the thumb of that former partner, and grow.

It all begins with forgiveness.

GET BEYOND YOUR EX, GET BEYOND YOURSELF, SEE THE BIG PICTURE

One of the biggest lessons I have learned in relating to my former wife is being taught to me by my current wife, Kathi. I was speaking at a church in a city where my youngest three sons were living at the time. Kathi was accompanying me, as was my oldest son, Jesse, who was providing the music for the event. My daughter, Joy, flew in for the weekend as well, so all five kids were there. My former spouse lived nearby, so she came to the church to see all her kids. I was okay with that—maybe a little uncomfortable—but okay.

After the morning service, Joy came up to me and said, "Dad, we have a little problem here."

"What's the matter?" I asked.

"Well, I know we said all the kids were going to have lunch with you and then dinner with Mom, but her plans have changed, and she's only available for lunch." She paused, took a deep breath, and dove in deeper. "Do you think we could have lunch with Mom and then have dinner with Kathi and you?"

Before I could answer, Kathi spoke up. "Why don't we all have lunch together?"

I turned to give her my most shocked facial expression. But on my way toward facing her, I focused on the look on my daughter's face. All the stress, all the tension seemed to miraculously and instantaneously disappear.

"That would be okay with you guys?" she asked in partial disbelief.

"Certainly," Kathi again responded, taking the lead. "It'll be fun."

Before I could register any form of protest, Joy scurried over to tell the rest of the family the good news.

"Can you see what's going on here, Bill?" Kathi inquired.

"What do you mean?"

"What I mean is that your poor kids are stressed out of their minds when their mom and dad are in the same room. They work hard to keep the two of you apart because they are afraid of how uncomfortable being together will make everyone. I say we try a little family healing with a little family togetherness."

I didn't see the wisdom in this decision immediately. Frankly, it was rather surrealistic to be seated at a restaurant with my children and my wives. But as the meal progressed, I could see more clearly what Kathi was talking about. The kids were laughing, telling stories on each other, and having a great time. Understand, this wasn't *The Parent Trap, Part Two* where the kids bring their divorced parents together in hopes of reconciliation. It was beyond that.

It was about the big picture of our family. We've made real progress in looking beyond ourselves, and it's been very rewarding.

I Will Trust God with My Life

One of the most basic concepts in the Scriptures is "Trust in the LORD with all your heart and do not lean on your own understanding" (Proverbs 3:5).

We can trust our futures to God. We can trust our children's futures to God. We trust God for our daily bread, our ability to pay our bills, our hope for good health, and a hundred other issues.

But can we trust God to give us the best possible relationship with our former mates?

Do you pray for him or her? What do you ask God to do? Ask the Lord to show you how *you* can make things better. Remember, you weren't put on earth to change your spouse, and you certainly weren't put here to change your ex-spouse! Take responsibility for what is yours, and commit the rest to the sovereign Lord, who gives us gifts that are good and perfect.

What's the location of the greatest spiritual lesson God wants you to learn? It could just be that "ex" marks the spot!

9

Dating May Be Different
When You're Not a Teenager

By DEFINITION, being a divorced person means you are without a spouse. This means we have an issue our married counterparts do not have to deal with—*dating*. I approach this topic with great exasperation, as I am painfully aware that I didn't do dating very well as a teenager, let alone as a middle-aged man. I feel inadequate writing about this subject. To be honest, one of my teenage sons set me up on my first date after I divorced! Me writing on dating feels like the Incredible Hulk giving ballet lessons.

My first date with Kathi, who is now my wife, is a classic example of how *not* to charm a woman, but she liked me anyway! I had met Kathi at a church I was speaking at in Southern California. I was able to have only a five-minute conversation with her after the meeting, but I boldly asked for her address and phone number, because I knew I wanted to ask her out.

In a remarkable display of God's grace, she gave me her information. Soon we began writing and calling—not much but enough to know both of us were interested.

A few weeks later I was back in her area, speaking at a corporate event at the Hilton Waterfront Resort in Huntington Beach. (Not just any event, either. I was keynoting the Food Shippers of America annual convention!) My presentation was at noon, so I asked her out for dinner that evening. She said yes, and I was as excited as a schoolboy.

I was also dumb as a schoolboy; I had neglected to handle a few key issues surrounding a successful date. Sheepishly I had to call Kathi to resolve my sloppy planning. "Kathi, there are a couple of things I need to ask you about our dinner," I said, trying to sound confident and competent, but I was neither.

"Sure, Bill. What's up?"

"Well," I stammered, "I really don't know Southern California restaurants, so I was wondering if you would mind picking out a place you'd like to go and making a reservation for us."

"Okay, I can do that," she replied without any indication whether she was disappointed in me or not.

"Thanks, Kathi. That would be a big help."

"Is there anything else I can do to help?" I could not believe how nice she was being to me. I was definitely taking note.

"Yes, actually there is one more thing." I was about to get *really bold.* If she was so understanding about choosing a restaurant, maybe this next request wouldn't sound lame either.

"What is it?"

"I feel a little foolish saying this," I began, "but the truth is, I flew into Southern California and took a cab from the airport to the hotel. So I don't have a car. I was wondering if you would mind driving…" Those last words just seemed to hang out there forever.

"No problem." She continued to sound so sweet.

"So can you pick me up around six?" I asked the question that was embarrassing beyond belief.

"I'll be there," was her reply.

"You drive; I'll buy!" was the worst retort I could have used. So, naturally, I used it.

She laughed. I winced. But God allowed a wonderful evening to take place.

Kathi picked me up right on time, just as she had promised. At the front of the hotel, I finally had a momentary flash of intelligence and offered to drive. I think she liked the idea, because she immediately agreed. Perhaps it was a glimmer of hope that all my brain cells were not dead.

We headed south on Pacific Coast Highway to a quiet little restaurant just beyond Laguna Beach. It was a wonderful choice. We were seated at a delightful table and given the menus. We small-talked at first—mostly about the entrées. The waiter returned, we ordered, he left, and suddenly we were on our own.

I knew this woman was special. It's the only reason I can offer for what transpired. Take note, dear reader, this is the tackiest tack a Turk can take on a first date. This explains in no uncertain terms why I had about one hundred first dates. Do not try this at home. Under normal circumstances this will blow up in your face.

I proceeded to fill the potentially awkward silence with the now-famous question, "Would you mind if I asked you a few questions about your personality?"

"Excuse me?" Kathi said, a bit taken aback.

"It's just a little personality profile I like to give people." I could see by her expression she had doubts about what was going on. "Relax," I said, trying to make it better but only making it worse. "There are no incorrect answers. You just respond with your preferences to the situations I describe. It'll be fun."

Fun like a root canal.

But she was a trooper. I plowed right into the Myers Briggs Type Indicator on my first date with my future wife. The only positive thing I can say about my behavior is that I resisted the urge to use the actual written test and chose instead to give it orally.

She answered all my questions and then asked me for the results of her test. Next she asked what my answers would have been. We laughed about our results—we were remarkably similar in most areas. (Years later I learned about a Myers Briggs phenomenon: people in first marriages tend to be very different in their answers, and folks in second marriages tend to be more similar.)

The rest of the dinner was a little more normal. We had such a good time that we lost all concept of time. We were the last couple to leave the restaurant at closing time. Yet we didn't want the evening to end. So where does a classy, godly man of integrity take his woman on a first date?

I took her to a hotel.

As scandalous as it sounds, it's true. Actually we drove to the Ritz Carlton in Laguna Niguel and sat in a wonderful room in their lobby called the Library. We ordered ginger ales from the lobby bar and continued talking for several more hours. It ended up being a rather lengthy first date, but we both knew we wanted to see each other again. And, as I have already told you, we grew in love and got married.

With that story as an introduction, it is mind-boggling to me that one of the questions I am most frequently asked when speaking at divorce recovery groups is, Do you have any advice regarding dating? This is far from the last word on dating, but perhaps some of these musings will help you sort through your situation.

ESTABLISH A HEALTHY IDENTITY

The old adage is still true: to find the right person you must be the right person. So many of us are on a quest to discover that perfect someone, but we forget to make sure our personal house is in order. For me, this means I need to have established a healthy identity, apart from the presence of a date, a girlfriend, or a wife.

Through my divorce I learned how easily I could wrap myself completely around one aspect of my life while neglecting other parts. When my marriage ended, I thought life was over. For others, a job or the kids or a love of reading or sports may completely consume their time. None of these in itself is bad. Just the opposite—they are all good. But it's the blending of these aspects that provides a healthy identity.

I like to work. I like to hang out with my family. I like to play golf, read books, and take walks. As long as I tap into all of these as a broad base in my life, I'm okay. A good way to measure my dependence on any of these items is to ask: if this aspect of my life was taken away, would I have something to fall back on? The answer indicates how unbalanced many of us can become. "If I lost my job, I'd go crazy!" you may say. Then you are too wrapped up in your job. "I don't know what I will do when my kids grow up and leave!" a proud parent may lament. Be careful of having too much of your life linked to your kids. They will grow up. They will leave home. That's the way God intended it to be.

If people tend to wrap themselves completely around one aspect of their lives, imagine the temptation to wrap themselves completely around their dates! If I'm saying things like "I'm *desperate* to find somebody to go out with," I'd better exercise some caution.

DEVELOP FRIENDSHIPS

Before venturing into the world of dating, it's important to know you have friends. Having a variety of friends is a wonderful way to expand your horizons. Married friends, single friends, male friends, and female friends create a nice mix.

Friends help us in a variety of ways. Not only can they assist with activities—picking up the kids from soccer practice, lending folding chairs for a party—but they also help meet our relational needs. When God said, "It is not good for the man to be alone," it was not meant exclusively as a marital pronouncement. We need each other, whether married or unmarried, romantic or nonromantic. We just need people in our lives.

This is vital in dating, because it helps answer the question, "Why am I dating in the first place?" If we're dating in order to develop friendships, that's fine, but our agenda may be viewed differently by the person we are dating. If we have a good group of friends around us, they can help sort out these issues.

Another way friends can help is by asking, "Are you even ready to date?" My best friend told me not long after my divorce, "You're *not* ready—not yet. You are so vulnerable right now that dating would be a big mistake."

"But I am so lonely," I confessed.

"I know," he replied, "but you've got 'rebound' written all over you right now."

"Rebound?"

"Yeah. You will fall for the first person you meet, whether she is right for you or not. You're anxious to medicate the pain of loneliness, so you'll jump right into something. It'll be quick, painless, and a *big* mistake."

Those were wise words I didn't want to hear, but I needed to hear them. That's why friends are important.

Go Slowly

Proceeding with caution in the world of dating sounds so simple, so basic that it's almost insulting to include it as a point to ponder.

Be insulted. Ponder it.

Speed dating is a tendency everyone faces. We are tempted to move a relationship ahead at the speed of light.

"Frank is the most wonderful man I've ever met," Ruth said to me during a recent conversation. "I'm smitten. I'm head over heels. This guy has won my heart."

"Wow," I replied with genuine interest. "This guy sounds like Mr. Perfect."

"He is," she responded with a huge sigh. "We're going to get married."

"No kidding?" I couldn't mask my surprise. "That's amazing, especially since I have never heard you talk about this guy until today. When did you guys meet?"

"Last Friday night."

"You met this guy less than a week ago, and you're getting married?"

"Well, he doesn't know we're getting married yet, but we both know the chemistry is off the chart. It will only be a matter of time before he proposes."

I never know quite what to do in a situation like this. Granted, I know lots of people who have fallen in love at first sight, so I realize it's a viable phenomenon. But experience tells me that more often than not, this is a formula for disaster. Frank and Ruth are moving way too fast, especially Ruth. The more I talked with her, the more I realized she was fairly new to dating. Her divorce had been finalized only two months earlier, and she was having a hard time dealing with a variety of issues. To me, it looked as though she was medicating her pain by bringing someone—anyone—into her life as quickly as possible. How much healthier it would have been for the two of them to slow down, get to know each other better, and proceed from there.

Ruth did get Frank to propose to her (I chose those words carefully). But the week of the wedding, Frank got cold feet and left town. Ruth was heartbroken all over again. Not everyone's story ends like this one. Some people go ahead and marry, only to discover uncharted issues once they are neck deep in a new marriage. I want to be fair—some couples find each other this way and stay together for the long haul. But I would consider them the exception rather than the rule.

The other issue that entangles a new relationship is moving too fast physically. In my mind the jury is still out on whether this is more difficult for hormone-charged teenagers or sexually experienced adults. Either way, we need to move slowly in our relationships so we don't have the additional issue of guilt feelings for going too far with our dates.

Work on the friendship in the beginning. There will be time for romantic involvement later. Make purity a priority. Make it a topic of discussion with the new person in your life.

So take it easy. Enjoy the life of a dating couple. Explore areas of life that are important to you, and discover what your new boyfriend or girl-friend feels about the same issues.

Know Your Nonnegotiables

I am not an advocate of a wish list, where you write down all the qualities the ideal man or woman would possess. In my view, doing so sets up an idealistic expectation to which no one will ever measure up. Or the opposite effect can occur when your wish list encourages you to ignore the other person's faults! But I do think it's a good idea to write down the qualities or issues in life you refuse to compromise on once you're involved in a relationship. Knowing your nonnegotiables in advance will spare you some pain in the future.

What kind of person do you want to date? If you don't know the answer to that question, you are in for a wild ride! Some folks like the spontaneity, intrigue, and mystery of a complete stranger, but if a relationship is going to develop, it's probably best to have guidelines in mind.

Are you looking for someone who is a Christian? Would you date a non-Christian? How about their kids? Would you date a man who has five kids? How about a woman who has no kids but looks forward to having lots of them in the future? Each person should think through such questions in advance. Even in middle age, it's easy to fall head over heels in love with someone, but if that someone doesn't share your value system, trouble could be brewing.

Remember, if you're a parent, your kids will figure into this equation as well. What do your kids think of the person you are dating? This is a tricky area, because we tend to put too much weight on the children's response. ("They love this guy, so I guess he must be the one" or "They hate her, so I guess I better dump her.") Dating is primarily about the other person and you, not the other person and your family. But family issues are important and should not be left out of the mix.

BE HONEST

As in any relationship, honesty is a virtue worth pursuing. Telling your date how you feel is an important aspect of integrity and trust in a growing couple. This is usually not difficult until we have to be honest about hard issues.

"I dated Bernie for six months," my friend Sandra told me during a recent phone conversation. "I thought we got along fine, but a problem was developing, and I knew I had to be honest with him."

"What was the problem?" I asked.

Sandra stammered a bit before finally opening up. "I knew Bernie was falling in love with me. I also knew I wasn't falling in love with him. I liked him, but I felt that we were supposed to be just friends."

"Did you tell him?" I gently prodded, knowing that "just friends" is a difficult concept to hear.

"Yes, I did," she whispered softly. "It broke his heart, but I had to be honest with him."

"How is he doing?"

"Okay," she replied. "We didn't talk for a while… I guess he needed a little distance, but lately he has started calling again. It appears that we have moved from a romantic relationship to a friendship."

I congratulated her on her honesty. Moving from a dating relationship to a friendship is awkward, and not all of us are capable of as smooth a transition as Sandra and Bernie made. But as painful as it was for Sandra to share her feelings with Bernie, it would have been much worse to be dishonest, "stringing him along" for fear of hurting him.

It goes back to why you're dating in the first place. It's probably wise to get issues like this one out on the table early in the dating process. If you're dating and you're only interested in a friendship, be clear about it. If you're looking for something more romantic and long term, be honest about that as well.

Another place for honesty is with our kids. Dating behind their backs usually comes back to haunt us. If your kids ask what you're doing, give them an honest answer. I was reluctant to tell my kids if I went out on a date, only to hear them sigh in relief. "Finally! Dad has a life! We were starting to wonder if you were ever gonna get out there again!"

SEEK GOD'S DIRECTION

If there was ever an issue that demands our sensitivity before the Lord, it is this one. "What do you want me to do, Lord?" is a question we should be asking in all aspects of life, including our dating.

I can still remember being a hormone-high teenager listening to a youth speaker try to talk sense into us high schoolers at church. We were more interested in the opposite sex than anything else in the whole wide world. He started talking about the beauty of marriage, the sanctity of marriage, God's design for marriage. But he added a caveat I have never forgotten: "Kids, don't expect a mate to do for you what only God can do for you."

I wasn't a kid anymore, but as a single-again I needed to hear that message more than ever. On those days when I felt inadequate, lonely, isolated, and so tired of life the way it was, my tendency was to think, "If only I had a wife, things would be different." Don't get me wrong; I am realistic enough to know that feelings like that are normal. But if I am expecting a future spouse to meet needs that only God can meet, I am missing a major part of my spiritual growth.

The apostle Paul said to the Philippians centuries ago: "Be anxious for nothing, but in everything by prayer and supplication with thanksgiving let your requests be made known to God. And the peace of God, which surpasses all comprehension, will guard your hearts and your minds in Christ Jesus" (Philippians 4:6–7).

In your regular prayer time, begin asking God to show you exactly what He has for you in terms of a future relationship. As He reveals it to you, be thankful for what He has done. His future for you may involve a new mate. It may not. The important thing is that He loves you more than you could ever be loved by another. Rest in His love. Relax. Take a chill pill. For the child of God who honestly puts his or her life in His hands, the message is clear:

He is faithful. Everything is going to be all right.

Part Four

The Ultimate

Issues

10

A Vital Skill:
Managing Change

THE PROCESS OF adjusting to life after divorce includes mastering a few key skills. None of them is more important than managing change. Most of us don't do well with change in general, and when a negative change occurs, it can be a major assault. And certainly a divorce qualifies as a negative change.

But if we can understand how change works, why we are frightened by it, how to deal with it, and God's perspective on it, we can stare down those negative issues and come out the victor!

We are in a far better place if we choose to accept change, since it's happening whether we accept it or not! Making friends with change can revolutionize our lives, not only assisting us in processing our divorces but giving us tools for all kinds of life issues.

THE PROCESS OF CHANGE

In the corporate world I am often invited to speak on the topic of change. Early in the presentation I try to get the audience to visualize a flow chart of life. Using eight words that all begin with the letter *c,* we walk through a typical passage in our worlds.

We always begin with *calm.* Most of us like the sound of that word, and it starts our journey in a positive way. We like to think of days that are orderly and scheduled, as opposed to days of upheaval. And in those descriptions we have a clue to why calm works for us.

We are calm because life is under our *control.* Things work out better when they are done the way we like them done. Control is a good thing, and the more of life that is under our control, the happier we tend to be.

But then it happens. We are faced with a fork in the road, and neither direction looks all that inviting. One side of the fork is a *crisis.* The other side is a *choice.* What disturbs us is that both directions lead us somewhere we really don't want to go—to *change.* I can choose to change, or I can wait for change to come upon me in some disastrous manner, but either way I have ended up in a noncalm, uncontrolled part of life that has produced something new—a change.

But the flow chart isn't complete. There are wonderful results of change if we are willing to follow it through. Change can produce *confidence.* We learn valuable lessons from change and consequently are better people for it.

Confidence on the outside often means we have deepened our *character* on the inside. Who hasn't been inspired by books, movies, or television shows about people who were dealt a difficult blow in life, yet they learned their lessons, fought back, and then were stronger and deeper than they would have been without the change.

And that brings us back to *calm*. Life returns to normalcy, if only for a little while. Change isn't always bad. Sometimes it can have a strong, positive influence on our lives.

Think about this flow chart and your current status of adjusting to your divorce. All was calm when you married, or at least that was the appearance you liked to present. Life was good because every aspect of it was under your control. I hope you can tell as you read that sentence that it really *wasn't* all that good, because you had become a bit of a control freak. Maybe that's why the next step occurred.

The next step was the divorce itself. Maybe you chose it, or maybe it was forced on you. Whether it was a choice or a crisis, when you were served with those papers, a radical change was about to take place.

But follow it through. Even though it was traumatic at the time, as you learn and grow and heal, you will gain a sense of confidence and deepen your character if you stay open to the lessons God wants you to learn. Don't dwell on the first part of the chart. We've all been there; it happened; it's time to move on. So focus on the latter part of the chart. What can we do to bring positive lessons into our lives as a result of our divorces? That sounds pretty good, doesn't it?

But it's still scary.

WHY CHANGE FRIGHTENS US

When most of us think about change, there is a jolt in our stomachs. It may be just the tiniest drip of stomach acid that creates a little churning or acid like huge waves in the ocean. Either way, change can be frightening. Why?

One reason is the *fear of the unknown.* We find ourselves thinking, *Better to fight the devil I know than the one I don't!* As horrible as those last few weeks or months were prior to our divorces, at least we had some idea of what to expect. It's not knowing what's ahead as single-agains that can be maddening. "I understand married life, but life on my own petrifies me. How will I meet other people? Who will help with my kids? How long will it take me to work through all this churning inside? Why is my former spouse treating me this way?" All these questions reflect our discomfort with change. They point to the fact that we like control, and divorce throws everything out of control. We liked our lives better when we were in charge, but those days are gone. Things have changed.

Another reason change frightens us is the *fear of failure*. Deep inside, we are still dealing with embarrassment over the fact that our marriages have failed. We find ourselves adding insult to injury by thinking, "What if I fail as a single? I didn't do marriage well, what assurance do I have that I'll do singleness well? Maybe I am exactly what my ex tells me I am—a big screwup!" None of us likes to fail, and the thought of it happening again can be paralyzing.

Fear of commitment is one more way change frightens us. This new lifestyle forces a big question: "What do I really want?" We say we want to learn and grow from the whole experience, but do we really mean it? "Do I want to remain single? Do I want to get into another relationship, knowing I open myself up to the same pain I'm desperately trying to get through right now?" Are we committed to change enough that we will work through the process, learning all that God has for us along the way? This kind of change forces us to zero in on our values, and that can be a daunting task.

Some of us fear change out of a *fear of disapproval.* If I change, I risk people saying they liked me better the way I was. Many of us who have endured divorce felt much better off, much more socially accepted, much more at peace with ourselves when we were happily or even unhappily married. Then, *bam,* the divorce happened, and we suddenly felt like outcasts of society. "I liked you better when you were married." Nobody says it, but it's there; you can sense it. We convince ourselves that people treated us better when we were married, so we are back to chapter 1 and a boatload of self-esteem issues.

Ironically, change can also bring a *fear of success.* I know it sounds backward, but for many of us the most paralyzing thought in the whole process is that we will successfully transition into an emotionally healthy single person. "I didn't like being single before I was married. I surely don't look forward to being single again after a marriage." So we self-destruct, intentionally sabotaging our own plan.

Maybe you identify with one of the reasons that causes us to fear change. Maybe you identify with several of them. The issue is, what can we do to make change our friend? Actually, we can take several steps. They all involve being more intentional about our lives, taking more command, and making more positive choices.

BEFRIENDING CHANGE IN OUR LIVES

Start with small, specific, limited goals in areas where you want to change. What can you do to begin moving closer to your ultimate goals? This sounds so basic, but many of us get tripped up from the outset. We decide we want to change, but we make our goals so grand that they are unattainable.

Maybe your ultimate goal is a new set of activities to take the place of some of the things you did as a married couple. The best way to approach that goal is to add a small thing to your daily routine. This might be the perfect time to take a class at the local community college or to read that book you have always wanted to read that is collecting dust on your shelf. This is a great opportunity to join a health club or go on that diet or start writing the mystery novel you've had in the back of your mind. But if you're going to add something to your daily routine, start with something realistic. You'll be busy before you know it!

Perhaps you don't want to give up those things you learned to enjoy. Well then, by all means continue to do them, but resolve to make new memories to replace the old ones that now are so painful. Maybe you enjoyed snow skiing as a couple. Your goal should be to enjoy snow skiing with new friends, forging new moments to treasure.

Proactive change will always be easier than reactive change. We have alluded to this point the entire chapter, so let's get it down in black and white. Change you can control will always be easier to handle than change that is forced upon you. If you knew a hurricane was headed for your home, it would be easier to choose to leave with some belongings than to wait for the winds and rain to hit. Either option involves radical change, but choosing to leave with some meaningful possessions is far superior to stubbornly waiting for the storm to force you out.

For example, if you know your divorce has affected your job performance, you have a choice. Either you decide to kick into gear and get back to the quality work you were known for in the past, or you wait for your pink slip. Ask yourself, how can I instigate change and possibly offset a reactive change?

Choose to stretch yourself. This is all about risk. Some people respond quite favorably to risk; the rest of us are scared. We can see it in our lives in dozens of ways. Several years ago I realized I have combed my hair the same way for decades. Part it down the left side; it almost fell into place naturally. My wife and some of my kids suggested I adopt a different hair style, a more contemporary one. I threw up all sorts of arguments. "I've always worn my hair this way! It was good enough for Abraham Lincoln! If I changed my haircut, it would be screaming midlife crisis!" But guess what happened? I tried it and liked it! People said I looked ten years younger (a good thing to say to someone my age). It doesn't take any time to comb—it's almost like the crew cut I got every summer as a child. The point is, a new hair style was a stretch for me. It was way-outside-the-box thinking for an I've-always-done-it-this-way guy. But now that I've done it, I'm glad I did. If it works that well with hair, think about your life! Go ahead. Take a risk. Stretch yourself.

Spread out the sources of your identity. If there was one change I needed to make after my divorce, it was to understand the dangers of mishandling this issue. We've discussed this topic already, but this change is so crucial to a healthy lifestyle, I believe it is worth reviewing. Let's begin with a question: have I wrapped myself completely around one aspect of my life? To best answer that question, consider it another way: if that one aspect were taken away from me, would I survive?

After my divorce, I realized how I had wrapped myself around my wife. I had neglected many other aspects of my life in order to devote myself fully to her. This is tricky, because I am not advocating the polar opposite response: neglecting a spouse. But I hadn't invested in friendships or hobbies or even my job, because I had been so focused on one aspect of my life—my marriage. So when it ended, I felt I was left with nothing. It's like the guy who's married to his job and then gets laid off. He's ready to jump off the thirteenth floor. Or the devoted mother who gives her entire life to her children only to find out they intend to grow up, move out, and get on with their lives as adults. The empty nest can be devastating to a mother who has no life beyond her children.

The answer is to spread out your sources of identity. I am more than a husband. I am a father. I am a worker. I am a friend. I am a golfer (loosely speaking). I am a lover of books. I am, most important, a child of God. Therefore, if I lose my spouse, my job, a child, or a friend, I will certainly feel the loss and grieve it, but I have a bit more equilibrium, because I have spread out my identity links.

Take care of yourself. If we aren't careful, we may be guilty of a typical fix for our pain—pouring our lives into somebody else. If I am taking care of another person, it distracts me from the personal work I need to do, especially at this critical time in my life. Although it sounds noble, even biblical, to help out a brother, don't allow that attitude to get in the way of your personal healing.

It's the familiar instruction from our friends the flight attendants. "Put your oxygen mask on first before helping others." Do I balance pleasing others with pleasing myself? It's okay to do work on your own behalf. It's not foolish or selfish or ultra-introspective. On the contrary, it's the right thing to do.

A PRESCRIPTION FOR CHANGE MANAGEMENT

Back in the early days of the Old Testament, there was a hero whom everyone knew and loved. His name was Moses. God handpicked him to take millions of Israelites out of bondage in Egypt and on to the Promised Land.

I have a hard time viewing Moses as a normal guy. In my mind, he is bigger than life. I'm old enough that when I visualize Moses, I see Charlton Heston.

But along the way to the Promised Land, some things happened, and

God saw fit not to allow Moses to enter it. Can you imagine the day that is described at the end of the book of Deuteronomy when Moses had the audacity to die!

All of a sudden there are big changes. The person you looked up to all those years is gone. And he's not coming back. This type of change didn't thrill the throng of millions, I am certain.

But let's make it even more personal, okay? You're not just any old Israelite in the middle of the masses. You are Joshua. And God is telling you to take over where Moses left off. How's that for a radical change? It's not a divorce, but there are certain similarities. The person Joshua had stood beside for years and years is suddenly out of the picture. Joshua had thoughts and dreams, and I imagine he shared them with Moses when the two hung out together. But all that is in the past. Joshua is on his own. He is faced with a big change, and I'm sure he is one scared pup.

So what does God tell Joshua to assure him that the change can be pulled off without incident? Actually, God tells Joshua three things, and we can use them today to make changes in our lives as well.

First, there is *God's promise.* In the first chapter of Joshua, God tells him:

Be strong and courageous, for you shall give this people possession
of the land which I swore to their fathers to give them. (Joshua 1:6)

"I will give you the land!" the Lord says to him. "It's a promise." He had promised the land to Abraham, and He had promised the land to Jacob. God promised it, and He was going to deliver.

And He has made promises to you as well. He has promised you eternal life. He has promised you abundant life. In Jeremiah 29:11 He has promised you "a future and a hope." That's change—positive change. And it's on its way, for the Lord promised it.

Second, there is *God's power*. His words to Joshua continue:

> Only be strong and very courageous; be careful to do according to
> all the law which Moses My servant commanded you; do not turn
> from it to the right or to the left, so that you may have success
> wherever you go. This book of the law shall not depart from your
> mouth, but you shall meditate on it day and night, so that you may
> be careful to do according to all that is written in it; for then you
> will make your way prosperous, and then you will have success.
> (Joshua 1:7–8)

"I will give you the strength to change!" God says.

God's power is in His Word, the Bible. For those of us who read these words, the Scriptures are our ultimate source of healing, encouragement, and energy. He gives us the power we need to make it day by day as we spend time reading, reflecting, and meditating on His Truth.

The thought of reading the Bible may be old hat for you, or it could be a totally new concept. Either way, I challenge you to make a change starting today for a positive tomorrow. Choose today to spend time each day reading His Word. The middle of the Bible is a wonderful place to hang out. It's a big book in the Old Testament called Psalms. Actually, they are lyrics to songs that were sung in those days, but you will find them rich with comfort, empathy, and solace. Through those words, God gives us the power we need to face the day. Try it. Maybe the best time for you is early in the morning or before bedtime or during the lunch hour at your workspace. Time and place don't matter. Just do it.

Finally God tells Joshua one more thing to help him make his changes, and I believe it is the most important promise. It is *God's presence.*

> Have I not commanded you? Be strong and courageous! Do not tremble or be dismayed, for the LORD your God is with you wherever you go. (Joshua 1:9)

"I will be with you through all your changes!" God says.

You don't ever have to feel all alone. God is with you always. Even though your former spouse left you, that's not the way God operates. He wants to embrace you and let you know that, together, the two of you can do anything. He knows you hurt. He knows you feel burned. He knows how reluctant you are to trust anyone again. He knows all about those feelings, and He just keeps reaching out His arms to hug you.

He has promised to see you through these days of change. He has offered to give you a daily power source by connecting to Him through His Word. And best of all, He promises to be with you wherever you go. It's the formula for successful change. All you have to do is put it into practice.

11

An Important Question: Where Is God?

I REALIZE THERE will be great variety in the backgrounds of those who read this book. And no place is that more noticeable than in our spiritual lives. You may have been brought up in church by godly parents who loved you and did everything humanly possible to see that you understood God's love, His sovereignty, His grace, and His forgiveness. Or perhaps you were brought up without a relationship with the Lord. Church was either something endured or completely absent from your early days. Or you may find yourself in between these two extremes.

But usually during a crisis most, if not all, of us start reflecting on spiritual issues. We want to make sense of life, even when it seems that the circumstances make no sense. In our despair or confusion, we will often turn our questioning to God.

"Where is God in my divorce?" is both a universal question and a personal one. All who have gone through divorce proceedings may ask that question, yet everyone has a unique set of circumstances revolving around that question. Consider these case studies.

MARTHA MEETS THE LORD

Martha was a good girl growing up. Her family placed doing the right thing above every other character quality in life. Like many people of their generation, Martha's parents looked at the church with cynical eyes. "They're a bunch of hypocrites," her dad would mutter. Consequently, church was not a part of Martha's life growing up.

After high school graduation, she went to another part of the state to go to college. She dated popular boys on campus and was nominated for homecoming queen her senior year. She met Aaron right before graduation at a sorority-fraternity social event. Aaron was tall, handsome, and full of ambition. He was headed to law school and looked forward to one day setting up his own law firm.

Martha and Aaron fell in love and soon married. She began working for an interior designer in town, helping put Aaron through law school. They were happy at first, but gradually things began a downward spiral. Martha, "the good girl," did all she could to hold the marriage together, but nothing seemed to work. Aaron had his sights on bigger and better things, and his future plans did not include Martha.

Martha spent the next few months with a variety of therapists, trying to make sense of what had just occurred. She gained much insight during this time of personal introspection, but there was still a nagging gap in her life. It was more than the absence of a husband. Something else was missing.

During this time an old friend from college showed up. Lucy hadn't seen Martha in years, but they reconnected, and soon Lucy got a sense of what was going on. After Martha filled in Lucy about her life, she turned the tables. "What's going on in your life?" she asked.

Lucy's reply would be life changing for Martha. "The biggest thing in our family's life is that we found a church in which we've become quite involved. It's warm, friendly, and caring. They have great programs for our kids, fascinating meetings for Jerry and me, and all kinds of other stuff on top of it all!"

Martha was a bit taken aback. She had never thought of Lucy as a churchgoer. "The church is having a concert tomorrow night," Lucy said. "Would you like to come?" Martha nodded yes.

At the concert, Martha saw what a church can be like when it's fully functioning. There were lots of friendly people, and the result was a winsome, almost contagious feeling. "After that concert, I was in the church building every time the doors were open," Martha now recalls. "The biggest commitment I made was signing up for a weekly Bible study."

There the leader, Donna, quietly befriended Martha. Several weeks into the study, the two women remained after the meeting, and Donna led Martha in a prayer in which Martha asked Jesus Christ to be her personal savior.

Martha grew spiritually over the next months. The "thing" that had been missing in her life all those years was actually the "person" named Jesus and His offer of a personal relationship.

"So where was God in my divorce?" she reflects. "I met the Lord *as a result* of my divorce, so I think the answer is pretty clear. I wouldn't want to go through all that pain and agony again, but I wonder how open to Lucy's invitation I would have been had I not gone through all that preceded it."

Martha's case seems to make sense regarding the "God" component in her life. Tom's case is more difficult to understand.

Tom, the Good Church Kid

Tom was born to wonderful Christian parents in a typical suburban town on the East Coast. From his earliest childhood memory, the small local church down the street was an integral part of his family's life. To any objective observer, the entire social life of Tom's family revolved around church activities. Tom recalls, "We went to church faithfully every Sunday morning and evening. They had a prayer meeting every Wednesday night, and we were there, too."

But that was just the beginning. Tom had Sunday school on Sunday morning, youth group on Sunday before the evening service, youth choir rehearsal on Monday nights, and Scouts on Tuesday night. He also helped a group from the church serve at a local rescue mission every Friday night.

"For some people, that's too much church," Tom reflects. "It turned off a lot of my peers. But I loved it. I had a healthy, growing devotion for the Lord and loved serving Him and others through my church."

Tom went off to the local university, majored in English, minored in education, and graduated four years later. He came back to his hometown to teach English at the same junior high school he had attended years earlier. But he brought back not only a degree but also his new wife, Francine. They had met in a creative writing class his junior year. Actually, he had seen her before that class—about two weeks earlier at a Campus Crusade event. Francine was a fellow believer, as deeply committed as Tom.

Theirs was a storybook marriage for quite some time. Children came along—three of them—and parenting brought a new set of challenges. But Tom and Francine managed to get through the parenting years without being worse for wear.

"Right before our thirtieth wedding anniversary," Tom recalls, "Francine just walked out. No note, no reasons, no explanation whatsoever. I was shocked, devastated—whatever word you want to use to convey a nuclear bomb going off in my world.

"I still had my teaching. I still had my kids. I still had friends at church. Looking back, I'm sure it could have been a lot worse. But the biggest issue to come out of my divorce was the question, God, why would You allow such a thing to happen in my life? From my perspective, I was a good guy, a good husband, father, and provider. But most of all I was a good Christian. I loved God. I dedicated my life to serve Him, and I tried to live like it every day. Why would this happen to me?"

WILLIS, THE WILD CHILD

Willis grew up in the polar opposite climate from Tom. His parents met at a rock concert in the sixties. They were classic hippies, heavily into drugs, sex, and rock-'n'-roll. Willis was born a few years after his parents moved in together, but his dad didn't stick around to see his son grow up.

"Without a father in my life, I did whatever I pleased," he recalls. "I was very messed up. I was messing around with girls when I was twelve, desperate to prove myself and get some attention."

But Willis had a life-changing experience in his senior year of high school. "A friend invited me to a meeting one night. There was singing and skits and lots of laughter. Then a guy sat on a stool up at the front and told us from the Bible how Jesus forgives all our sins. I knew I was a pretty major sinner, so I paid close attention. He gave us an opportunity to receive the Lord as our Savior, so I did it!"

Life changed radically for Willis. He started hanging around Christian friends, and before long he was off drugs and living a life of purity. It was at this time he met Jan. They dated all through college and married soon after graduation. Active in their church, they volunteered to help the high school pastor lead the kids in their activities.

Somewhere along the way, Willis allowed his spiritual life to wane. He began going through the motions. The Lord wasn't real in his life. He became increasingly disillusioned by the church and eventually stopped going. At this stage in their marriage, trouble erupted. Jan continued going to church every Sunday, and while she was there, Willis started meeting a woman he'd met at the gym for "breakfast." It turned into a full-blown affair, and ultimately Willis filed for divorce.

"Where was God?" he asks today. "At the time I didn't care. It didn't matter to me. I wanted my own way, and God was just gonna have to deal with it!"

HOLLY'S UNPLEASANT SURPRISE

Holly was a good Southern lady from the time she was too young to be called a lady. Something about her Southern drawl, the polite "yes ma'am" and "no sir," and the charm and grace of Southern hospitality made Holly the perfect catch. And there was a male version of Holly, whom she found immensely attractive. Barry was a polite Southern gentleman who made a positive impression on everyone. Barry and Holly were an ideal match, and they knew it. After dating in high school, they married in the summer between their sophomore and junior years of college.

Their marriage began in the storybook fashion one would expect. Not only were they young and attractive, they also came from rather affluent families, so money flowed freely from both sources. Barry finished his business degree and settled into an upper-management position in his father's company, while Holly completed an art degree and began designing greeting cards for a national stationery company.

The change in their marriage was so miniscule that Holly didn't even notice it at first. "I knew Barry was under a fair amount of pressure at work," she now reflects. "He lived under constant deadlines, and he didn't do well under that stress."

Barry began spending more and more time at the office, away from Holly. She had no reason to be suspicious. She trusted Barry completely. But Barry wasn't being honest with his wife. There were lots of long hours, to be sure, but not as many as he led her to believe. He stayed out a great deal of the time, working on a new passion in his life—drinking. Several young, good-looking co-workers were more than willing to accompany Barry to a bar after work, and he enjoyed the attention that came with it.

Over time these unhealthy patterns ran their course. Not only had Barry become addicted to alcohol, he had also engaged in multiple affairs with his co-workers. He became cold and aloof to Holly. Eventually Barry felt he had found a new love at work, and he filed papers, leaving his wife in an ocean of questions.

"How could this have happened?" Holly asks. "He was the perfect guy from the perfect family. He grew up in church and had, to all who could observe, a genuine personal relationship with the Lord. How could he move in such a different direction? I was good to him; he had no reason to be unhappy or dissatisfied with me! And where was God while all this was happening? It just doesn't make any sense."

My background was similar to Holly's and Tom's in that the church was a vital part of my growing-up years. I knew about the Lord Jesus early in life, and by high school I had dedicated my life to ministry. I graduated from Bible college and seminary totally committed to serving God wherever He put me.

When my marriage ended, it felt like the world stopped. I have chronicled my personal pain and heartache throughout this book, but, interestingly enough, I can say with total honesty that I never questioned God's sovereign control of the entire situation. Was I angry? Yes, but not at God. All of us respond in our unique and individual ways when situations present themselves, and that is precisely my point.

THEOLOGY 101

I don't have all the answers—far from it. But I know God does, and even when it makes no sense to me, God has a plan. Perhaps it would be helpful to review some basic teaching from the Bible in order to give perspective to your individual situation. You may not think this is pretty, but you need to consider it as you seek to make sense of the circumstances that currently surround your life.

According to the way most people understand the Bible, when two people marry, they are entering a covenant with each other and with God, and the extent of that covenant is for life. "For this reason a man shall leave his father and his mother, and be joined to his wife; and they shall become one flesh" (Genesis 2:24).

Therefore, if two people divorce, they have violated that covenant, and that would be viewed as a sin. (Now don't get angry at me—I'm on your side—but it's vital to understand God's perspective on this issue.) "When you make a vow to God, do not be late in paying it; for He takes no delight in fools. Pay what you vow! It is better that you should not vow than that you should vow and not pay" (Ecclesiastes 5:4–5).

At this point much of the interpretation becomes very personal in our world today. Specifically, some folks view all sin as sin, without rank or distinction. Others, however, tend to give weight to certain sins above others. It's not good that you cheat on your taxes, but at least you're not gay, which is far worse. Or, I have no desire to curb my sin of gluttony (eating like a pig at the church socials), but at least I'm not divorced, which is far worse. Or, I gossip all over town about others' extramarital affairs, but at least I am faithful to my spouse.

I think I've made my point. For our purposes, we simply need to understand that divorce is a sin. As with any other sin, we are invited by God to come to Him and ask for forgiveness, and He promises to cleanse us. (Remember all we covered in chapter 6.) "If we confess our sins, He is faithful and righteous to forgive us our sins and to cleanse us from all unrighteousness" (1 John 1:9).

So why did God allow your divorce to take place? For the same reason He allows murders, overeating, and gossip. Once Adam and Eve freely chose to disobey God in the Garden of Eden, sin entered the world. Even all these centuries later, you and I have our choice, or free will, to decide how we will live.

With the entrance of sin into the world, there also came suffering. It is far from a perfect world, and for many of us, the strongest realization of this truth is the dissolution of our marriages. So why does God allow pain and suffering in our world? The Bible speaks of at least three possible reasons. One would be called natural consequences. We reap what we sow. "Do not be deceived, God is not mocked; for whatever a man sows, this he will also reap" (Galatians 6:7).

If I foolishly jump off my ladder and land awkwardly on my foot, the natural consequence will be the pain of a broken ankle. It just makes sense. Maybe you married someone whom you knew better than to marry. Did you expect God to supernaturally intervene from the sky, screaming, "Don't marry that person"? That's not the way God operates, and you know it. He allowed you to make your choice.

Another reason for suffering is our own mistakes. "For what credit is there if, when you sin and are harshly treated, you endure it with patience?" (1 Peter 2:20).

When we sin, we pay the price. Why did our marriages fall apart? Perhaps our own shortcomings and irresponsibility come to the forefront. It is not accurate to pin the blame on God for sexual unfaithfulness or mental abuse or drinking problems or anger issues. We chose our paths, and we see the consequences played out in life.

But there is a third reason for suffering mentioned in the Scriptures. We suffer simply for being a Christian. "For it is better, if God should will it so, that you suffer for doing what is right rather than for doing what is wrong" (1 Peter 3:17).

For some of us, this provides solace in our pain. Sure, we were not without fault in our marriages, but we honestly attempted to address the issues that were causing its breakdown. We wanted our marriages to last. We didn't want them to go away. God asks us to learn from our suffering and to move ahead in our lives.

As I write these words, I am thinking of many men and women I have met all over North America in the last twelve years who have tried to make theological sense of their divorces. For some it comes easy, but for others it still doesn't make sense after many years. God's ways are higher than our ways, He tells us in the Old Testament, and this circumstance may be an illustration of that very truth. You may never understand the why behind your divorce until you get to heaven and are able to ask Him yourself.

With these theological principles in mind, perhaps some of the case studies earlier in the chapter can make more sense. Or maybe they don't. It is a daunting task to attempt to understand the mind of God. But I can assure you, He wants the very best for you.

Recently I discovered a small phrase tucked away in Psalms that has come to mean so much to me: "He rescued me, because He delighted in me" (Psalm 18:19).

Even though many questions may never be answered, of one thing we are certain: God's love is unending. He delivered us from the ultimate effects of our sin, because He takes great delight in us. He loves you, dear friend, right now, no matter how bright or grim the circumstances may be. The effects of your divorce are not God's being mean to you. He is good, perfect, and righteous. He cares about you deeply. Allow Him to delight in you.

12

A New Beginning:
The Promise of
the Second Wind

WHEN LIFE DOESN'T turn out the way we planned, there is a danger we will give up hope that life will ever be pleasant again. All of us have had those feelings at some point, but it doesn't have to be that way. Good news is on the way.

A few years ago I wrote a book along with my friend Dean Merrill that we titled *The Promise of the Second Wind: It's Never Too Late to Pursue God's Best.* The premise for the book was born out of my own experience. Allow me to give you the Cliffs Notes version of that book in this final chapter.

The metaphor of the second wind came from my experiences while running on the beach near my home in Southern California. Since I had never been a runner, the very thought of doing anything faster than walking was mind-boggling. But I made a radical decision several years ago to lose weight by eating healthy foods and exercising, and it appeared that running on the beach was a form of exercise that was tolerable to me.

The truth is, I began by walking on the beach, close to the water, on the wet sand. Wearing my trademark gray T-shirt so I could fully appreciate the drowning sweat I would work up, I made my way down the sand.

Ultimately I would come to a place where I felt I could increase the pace from a walk to a run. That's when the pains began in earnest. First, they were individual, localized pains, appearing one at a time. My thighs would start screaming. Then my lungs would feel like they were exploding. My eyelids hurt. One by one the pains arrived.

But the next phase was the most brutal. Suddenly all the individual pains came together in one grand, glorious chorus. Everything that could hurt did hurt. Runners refer to this phenomenon as "hitting the wall." I hit it, and I hit it hard. Right there, in the shadow of the Forty-fourth Street lifeguard stand, I was overcome with such intense pain that I had to end my running and finish my time by walking.

I would not give up, however. The next thing I knew, I experienced one of the most exhilarating moments of my life. One day not too long after I had first hit the wall, I hit it again at Forty-fourth Street. But through the pain, I felt a boost of energy, a revitalizing of my body and spirit. I was running through the wall of pain. Runners call it "getting your second wind."

It's a scientific phenomenon. Researchers have studied marathoners and have discovered that in the twenty-six-mile run most participants hit the wall at the twentieth or twenty-first mile. But most still finish the event. How is that possible? They experience their second wind.

The first time I caught my second wind, you would have thought I was Rocky on the steps of the art museum in Philadelphia. I was totally pumped!

I began sharing my experience with my friends, and everyone seemed to resonate with it. At that point I realized that in this running phenomenon I had experienced a wonderful metaphor for my life. I had started running my race and had done quite well for a fairly long distance. Then I hit the wall. I got divorced.

I didn't think I would ever be happy again. But the good Lord has given me my second wind. I am happier than I have ever been. What I thought could never happen has happened.

When Do You Need a Second Wind?

The nice thing about a second wind is that it is for all of us. You're not too young for a second wind; you're not too old. You're not too rich or too poor. It's not based on gender, socioeconomic status, or lineage. You can't say you're too inexperienced or too flawed or too set in your ways or too beat-up.

When do you need a second wind? Whenever you have hit the wall! Certainly a divorce qualifies as a hit-the-wall experience. But a wall can include myriad other circumstances. A wall in your life can be dealing with a medical issue for you or a family member. It can be a financial struggle. It can be a rebellious child. It can be the loss of a job or the death of a dear friend.

But the wall in your life can be more private and personal as well. It could be dealing with *disappointment,* as you find yourself saying, "I didn't think it would turn out this way." Or perhaps it's *regret,* saying, "I wish I had done things differently." Maybe your wall is *failure:* "I just blew it completely in a particular area of my life."

The wall in your life could be *frustration,* which says, "I feel so unsettled; I'm just churning inside." *Confusion* is another wall. "It should have worked. I can't understand why it didn't." Or, more seriously, perhaps *depression* is your wall. "I'm sad—all the time—about everything."

Maybe *lethargy* or *fatigue* has become your wall. "I've lost my energy for life." Or *isolation,* which says, "I've been burned once, so I've learned my lesson. I'm not going to expose myself to that kind of pain ever again. I don't need anybody, and nobody needs me." The wall in your life could be *fear* or *anxiety,* which says, "I'm scared!"

Or maybe the wall in your life is that you have *lost the ability to dream.* "Why should I dream? My dreams never come true!" Or life is *no fun.* "It's the same ol' boring routine." Worst of all, the wall in your life could be that you have *lost hope.* You have convinced yourself in your heart of hearts that even God isn't interested in you anymore.

Life is a marathon, and the need for a second wind comes to every one of us in a variety of contexts. But it does come.

WHAT DOES A SECOND WIND LOOK LIKE?

A second wind is as personal as the walls in our lives. For some of us, a second wind is the promise of a *renewed purpose* in our lives. We have been through such deep waters the last few months due to this divorce that we have veered off course. "I know why I am here," is a statement we long to make with clarity and conviction.

Some of us know why we're here, but we want to take it a step further by saying, "I know where I'm going." The second wind can offer us a sense of *reenergized direction.*

For a whole host of brothers and sisters who read these words, their divorces have simply worn them out. The thought of *revitalized energy* is a promise that sounds too good to be true. The second wind can offer fresh fuel for running life's race.

How Do I Get a Second Wind?

Two years ago when I set out to study characters from the Bible who experienced a second wind, I was hoping to uncover a formula that they all used to attract the second wind. But to my dismay, Moses's second wind was quite different from Zechariah's and Elizabeth's second wind. God dealt with Joshua differently than Jonah. The disciples experienced a second wind, as did the woman taken in adultery recorded in John's gospel, yet they were all treated uniquely.

I must admit that at first this really threw me. Now I wasn't able to say to people, "Do you want the second wind in your life? Well, step right up! If you will do A and B and C, you, too, will experience the second wind! That'll be twenty-five cents, please!"

So there is not a formula to apply in order to experience a second wind. But we can make some general observations. If we can put ourselves in the path of these seven principles, we are in the best place possible to take advantage of the second wind.

Be Proactive

The metaphor of the second wind can almost make it sound so supernatural that we conclude if we will just lie in bed, God will ultimately zap us while we're in the fetal position under the covers. No, the Lord created the laws of inertia and knows it is always easier to direct a moving object.

Your divorce was likely a debilitating blow. We have talked about the need to give yourself time and distance to allow God to heal your soul. How much time? It's a case-by-case call. But I must warn you, there will be a tendency to hide behind such information to justify a bad case of lethargy or fatigue. We all have to reach the point where we pick ourselves up, dust ourselves off, and get back in the race.

In the New Testament, for example, James tells us about being pro-active: "But prove yourselves doers of the word, and not merely hearers who delude themselves" (James 1:22).

Don't just read the Word; act on it. Don't just sit there; do something. It's a fine balance—the biblical imperative to "wait on the Lord" juxtaposed with getting out there and doing something. It's tricky and very personal, but it's a balance you need to work toward achieving. When a runner hits the wall, the overwhelming desire is to stop running, just quit right on the spot. But can you see what the runner would miss if he or she didn't run through the pain to experience the next phase of life's race. If I had quit and missed out on the wonderful life I have now, it would have been a tragedy.

Face Your Giants

I may be guilty of switching metaphors here, but for some, a giant is easier to visualize than a wall. Someone or something has come into your life and robbed you of your joy. It may be feelings of guilt or inferiority or jealousy or lust. It may be that you believe people look at you differently now that you are divorced. It may be a financial giant or an ulcer you've developed or a dozen other possibilities. Just like Goliath of the Old Testament, your giant is big, brash, and intimidating and has no concept of God's plan in all that has occurred.

And you feel like David—young, inexperienced, wet-behind-the-ears

David. If there had been Vegas-style betting back then, all the money would have been on Goliath. But David had a secret weapon that enabled him to face his giant. He had God on his side!

> Then David said to the Philistine, "You come to me with a sword, a spear, and a javelin, but I come to you in the name of the LORD of hosts, the God of the armies of Israel, whom you have taunted. This day the LORD will deliver you up into my hands." (1 Samuel 17:45–46)

David understood that his power came from the Lord. Fast-forward to modern days. When my life came crumbling down, I recognized quickly that my divorce was my giant and that I was allowing it to beat me into the ground. I also realized that I was too small on my own to take it on.

But God still works in lives today. He helped me face the most difficult circumstance I had ever encountered and come out a victor. Granted, since my faith was weaker than David's, I have more battle scars than he did, but I used the same approach—trusting my Lord—and achieved the same victory.

Make the Right Choices

Adjusting to life as a single-again can be a topsy-turvy process. Things that we once valued and gave priority to can get lost in the shuffle if we are not careful. More than once we've seen good people go bad due to traumatic circumstances in their lives.

But one constant through all of life is *right is right.* I am not fooling anyone if I knowingly go the wrong way. "It's been a rough year," we attempt to rationalize. "I'm trying new things. I'm experimenting with new ideas." If all of that ends up being code for "I've chucked my moral compass, and now I'm doing what I darn well please," Houston, we have a problem.

If we want to be at the place in life's race where God can reenergize us with His second wind, we've got to follow the path of right. Plenty of areas in life are gray, but plenty of issues are black or white. Don't tempt yourself by choosing the wrong way. The old adage "It's never wrong to do right" should end up on an index card and hung on your fridge or bathroom mirror or cubicle at work. Solomon, the Bill Gates of his day, tells us that doing right is even better than the big bucks! "He who trusts in his riches will fall, but the righteous will flourish like the green leaf" (Proverbs 11:28).

Take Your Stand

But the plot thickens. Once you determine you are going to do what is right, you will be constantly tested on your resolve. "I know what's right and I know what's wrong in this particular situation," we tell ourselves. "But I think God will understand if I go the wrong way just this once." That sort of thinking will get us into big-time trouble.

The apostle Paul understood our tendencies when he wrote to the Galatians: "It was for freedom that Christ set us free; therefore keep standing firm and do not be subject again to a yoke of slavery" (Galatians 5:1).

"This is my biggest area of struggle," my friend Ava confesses. "After my divorce, I went through all the right exercises to heal. I saw a professional counselor, I got involved in an ongoing divorce recovery group, I plugged into my local church, I attended a weekly Bible study and even created my own personal accountability group. I feel as though I jumped through all the right hoops.

"So when the time was right, I slowly reentered the world of dating.

And I have to tell you, I was shocked. From my perspective, no men out there met my personal criteria for a future mate. Consequently, I went quite a long time without a date.

"One day at my accountability group, we began talking about my dating dry spell. It was at that point that one of the women suggested I was setting my standards too high and I needed to lower them. I respected her counsel and did what she said.

"Now the problem is a different one. I have dates, actually lots of them. But the guys I date aren't on the same page as I am, especially spiritually. It's getting complicated because I am growing very close to a guy named Don, who has little spiritual interest."

Ava's battle is another one with which we are all familiar. What do I do about setting my sights on a future mate? Having already discussed this issue in an earlier chapter, let me just suggest that dating is a good place to take your stand. Don't back down. If it is God's will, He will bring someone to you who will be the person of your dreams—and His dreams for you!

Learn the Lessons in Waiting

Ava's story continues. She broke off the relationship with Don, which was not easy to do. Like any of us, she went through a lot of second-guessing after the breakup, especially when her dating seemed to dry up completely.

"I was in a holding pattern, like a plane circling the airfield but not able to land," she recalls. "And for a while, all I could think about was landing my plane."

I shared with her that when I was in the identical stage, I decided to do a word study in the Bible. I looked up every place in the Bible where God used the word *wait*. It was one of the most enlightening exercises I ever experienced. For instance, look at David's words in Psalm 37:

Rest in the LORD and wait patiently for Him;

Do not fret because of him who prospers in his way,

Because of the man who carries out wicked schemes.

Cease from anger and forsake wrath;

Do not fret; it leads only to evildoing.

For evildoers will be cut off,

But those who wait for the LORD, they will inherit the land.

     (Psalm 37:7–9)

Ava took my advice and did her own study on waiting. She discovered what I discovered: God will teach us valuable lessons in our times of waiting. I had to come to grips with my singleness. "God, if you want me to remain single the rest of my life, I accept that as your plan," was the big lesson God had for me. In Ava's case, she is still waiting. But in that season, she is finding great comfort, even delight in learning more about her heavenly Father and His unfailing love for her.

Appreciate God's Good Gifts

There is a wonderful verse in the book of James: "Every good thing given and every perfect gift is from above, coming down from the Father of lights, with whom there is no variation or shifting shadow" (1:17).

When we think about God's good gifts in our lives, we naturally think of the good things we have experienced in life: a good job, great children, fine friends, financial blessings.

But some of us have been around the track of life long enough to know that even the stuff we consider not good can ultimately be considered one of God's good gifts. I am not ready to call my divorce a good gift, but I am very clear that all I learned as a result of my divorce is a good gift. And I would not have met my sweet wife Kathi if life hadn't taken this curve in the road. It's just as we discussed in the chapter on change. My personal change came as a result of a crisis. I didn't ask for it, but God allowed it and used it to teach me lessons that have deepened my character. And the longer I live, the more I appreciate what He has given me, both the good and the stuff I didn't think was good at the time.

Be Available

The one constant in the Scriptures regarding the second wind is that God gives it to us when we make ourselves available for it. We don't have to pass a rigorous test of character strengths. We don't have to have a certain level of financial success. We don't have to jump through any hoops, actually. It's not about abilities; it's about availability.

In the Old Testament, God was looking for someone to do big things. He found the right person in a man named Isaiah: "Then I heard the voice of the Lord, saying, 'Whom shall I send, and who will go for Us?' Then I said, 'Here am I. Send me!'" (Isaiah 6:8).

"Here am I!" Is that the cry of your heart today? Deep inside, do you find yourself saying, "Lord, forgive me for the messes I have made in my life. I want a fresh start. I want a new beginning. I want a second chance." How is it going to happen? By making ourselves available to Him. He will take us, clean us up, teach us lessons along the way, and get us back in the race of life.

What I'm saying is true, because it is what God offers you. All you need to do is trust Him. One day at a time. Step by step. Try it, you'll see. You can have...

A fresh start.

A new beginning.

A second chance.

The title of this chapter is true. You can have the promise of the second wind. And the title of this book is equally true. You can have *new life after divorce*.